Dinah Zike's

Big Book of
World History

Middle School and High School

Dinah Zike, M.Ed.

Copyright 2007, Dinah-Might Adventures, LP
Dinah-Might Adventures, LP
P.O. Box 690328
San Antonio, Texas 78269-0328

Office (210) 698-0123
Fax (210) 698-0095
Orders only: 1-800-99DINAH (993-4624)
Orders or catalog requests: orders@dinah.com
E-mail: dma@dinah.com
Website: www.dinah.com
ISBN 13: 978-1-882796-25-0
ISBN 10: 1-882796-25-X

Table of Contents

Graphics

Index

Dear Teacher:

What is a Foldable?

In this book you will find instructions for making Foldables as well as ideas on how to use them. A Foldable is a 3-D, interactive graphic organizer. Making a Foldable gives students a fun, hands-on activity that helps them organize and retain information.

I first began inventing, designing, and adapting Foldables over thirty-five years ago. Today, I present Foldable workshops and keynote addresses to over 50,000 teachers and parents a year. Students of all ages are using my Foldables for daily work, note-taking activities, student-directed projects, as forms of alternative assessment, journals, graphs, charts, tables, and more. You may have seen at least one of the Foldables featured in this book used in supplemental programs or staff-development workshops.

After workshop presentations, participants would often ask me for lists of activities to be used with the Foldables they had just learned to make. They needed help visualizing how Foldables could be used to display the data associated with their disciplines—in this case, World History. So, over twenty-five years ago, I started collecting and sharing my ideas about how Foldables could be used to meet the needs of the World History teacher.

This book is the fruit of those years. It is organized in three parts. The first part introduces Foldables, explaining how they work and some of the ways they can be used. The second part gives step-by-step instructions on how to make 35 basic Foldable activities, along with practical classroom-tested tips. Finally, the third part of the book presents suggestions for using Foldables with specific World History topics.

Workshops
Contact Jeanne Herbes
1-210-698-0123
jeanne@dinah.com

Orders
1-800-99DINAH
orders@dinah.com
www.dinah.com

E-Group
Join on website:
www.dinah.com
or e-mail mindy@dinah.com

Why use Foldables in World History?

When teachers ask me why they should take time to use the Foldables featured in this book, I explain that they

. . . quickly organize, display, and arrange data, making it easier for students to grasp world history concepts, theories, facts, opinions, questions, research, and ideas. They also help sequence events as outlined in the content standards.

. . . result in student-made study guides that are compiled as students listen for main ideas, read for main ideas, or conduct research.

. . . provide a multitude of creative formats in which students can present projects, research, interviews, and inquiry-based reports instead of typical poster board or social studies fair formats.

. . . replace teacher-generated writing or photocopied sheets with student-generated print.

. . . incorporate the use of such skills as comparing and contrasting, recognizing cause and effect, and finding similarities and differences into daily work and long-term projects. For example, these Foldables can be used to compare and contrast student explanations and/or opinions to explanations and/or opinions currently accepted by experts in the field of social studies.

. . . continue to "immerse" students in previously learned vocabulary, concepts, information, generalizations, ideas, and theories, providing them with a strong foundation that they can build upon with new observations, concepts, and knowledge.

. . . can be used by students or teachers to easily communicate data through graphs, tables, charts, models, and diagrams, including Venn diagrams.

. . . allow students to make their own journals for recording observations, research information, primary and secondary source data, surveys, and more.

. . . can be used as alternative assessment tools by teachers to evaluate student progress or by students to evaluate their own progress.

. . . integrate language arts, the sciences, and mathematics into the study of world history.

. . . provide a sense of student ownership or investment in the world history curriculum.

National Social Studies Standards and Communication Skills

The National Social Studies Standards stress the importance of communication skills in social studies education. Not all students will become government officials, geographers, or historians, but all students need to be able to think, analyze, and communicate using social studies skills. Throughout their lives, students will be called upon to be social studies literate as they make observations, analyze and recall empirical data, read and differentiate between fact and opinion, discuss pros and cons of actions and reactions, justify voting for or against an issue, research a topic related to their well being or interests, make cause-and-effect decisions about their actions, write editorials to express their views publicly, and more. Foldables are one of many techniques that can be used to integrate reading, writing, thinking, debating, researching, and other communication skills into an interdisciplinary social studies curriculum.

Foldable Basics

What to Write and Where

Teach students to write general information--titles, vocabulary words, concepts, questions, main ideas, and dates--on the front tabs of their Foldables. General information is viewed every time a student looks at a Foldable. Foldables help students focus on and remember key points without being distracted by other print.

Ask students to write specific information—supporting ideas, student thoughts, answers to questions, research information, empirical data, class notes, observations, and definitions—under the tabs.

As you teach, demonstrate different ways in which Foldables can be used. Soon you will find that students make their own Foldables and use them independently for study guides and projects.

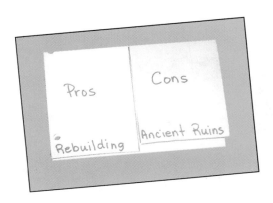

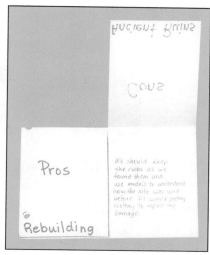

With or Without Tabs

Foldables with flaps or tabs create study guides that students can use to self check what they know about the general information on the front of tabs. Use Foldables without tabs for assessment purposes (where it's too late to self check) or projects where information is presented for others to view quickly.

Venn Diagram used as a study guide

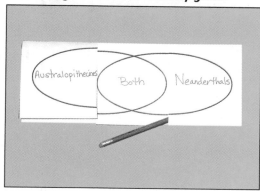

Venn Diagram used for assessment

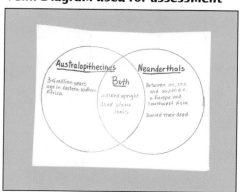

What to Do with Scissors and Glue

I do not ask middle school and high school students to carry glue and scissors from class to class. Instead, I set up a small table or rolling cart in the back of the classroom and provide a few containers of glue, several pairs of scissors (sometimes tied to the cart), containers of colored pencils, a stapler, and anything else I think students might need. Don't be surprised if students donate colored markers, decorative-edged scissors, gel pens, stencils, and other art items to your cart

The more they make and use graphic organizers, the faster students become at producing them.

Storing Graphic Organizers in Student Portfolios

Turn one-gallon freezer bags into student portfolios which can be collected and stored in the classroom. Students can also carry their portfolios in their notebooks if they place strips of two-inch clear tape along one side and punch three holes through the taped edge.

Have each student write his or her name along the top of the plastic portfolio with a permanent marker and cover the writing with two-inch clear tape to keep it from wearing off.

Cut the bottom corners off the bag so it won't hold air and will stack and store easily.

HINT: *I found it more convenient to keep student portfolios in my classroom so student work was always available when needed and not "left at home" or "in the car." Giant laundry-soap boxes make good storage containers for portfolios.*

Let Students Use This Book As an Idea Reference

Make this book of lists available to students to use as an idea reference for projects, discussions, debates, extra credit work, cooperative learning group presentations, and more.

Using Visuals and Graphics with Foldables

I designed the reproducible graphics in this book to be used as visual aids for student production, while immersing students in measurement, percentages, maps, and time lines. At times, I require these graphics to be used in student presentations. I photocopy them or print them from my computer and pass them out. At other times, students incorporate them into their journals, notes, projects, and study guides independently. I found that students and teachers were more likely to use graphics if they were available on a classroom computer where they could be selected and printed out as needed.

1. Mark and label maps to show where past and recent events occurred, where a historic person lived and worked, where wars were fought and battles won, where boundaries of territories or regions existed, etc.

2. Hundreds grids can be used to illustrate percentages, decimals, and bar graphs.

3. Use time lines to record when someone lived or when an event or sequence of events occurred. Use two time lines to compare what was happening in two different areas at the same time.

4. Use small picture frames to sketch or name a person, place, or thing. Great to use with the four-door book as a "who, what, when, where" activity.

5. Use thermometers in projects to show average seasonal temperatures of a geographic area

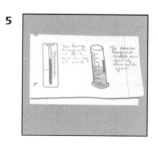

NOTE: *I grant you permission to photocopy page 4 and place copies of them in the production center or publishing center of your classroom. I also grant you permission to scan these pages and use them electronically.*

Temperature Gauges

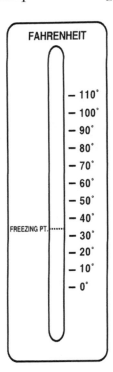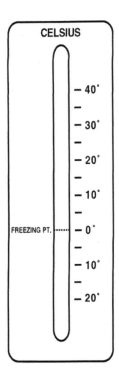

Rain Gauge

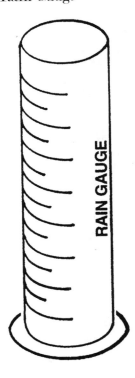

Picture Frame

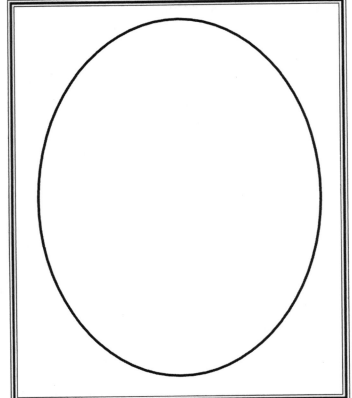

Hundreds Grid

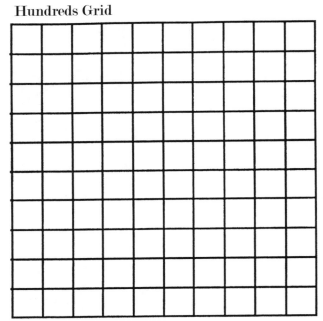

Basic Foldable Shapes

The following figures illustrate the basic folds that are referred to throughout the following section of this book

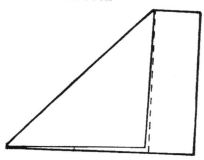

Taco Fold

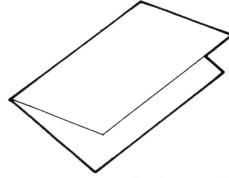

Hamburger Fold

Hot Dog Fold

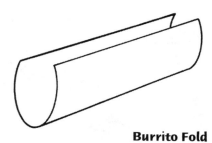

Burrito Fold

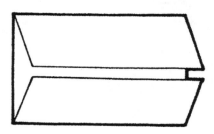

Shutter Fold

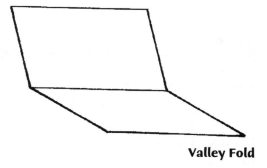

Valley Fold

Mountain Fold

Half-Book

Fold a sheet of paper (8 1/2" χ 11") in half.

1. This book can be folded vertically like a *hot dog* or . . .

2. . . . it can be folded horizontally like a *hamburger.*

Use this book for descriptive, expository, persuasive, or narrative writing, as well as graphs, diagrams, or charts.

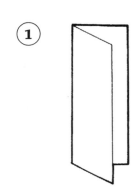

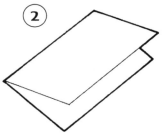

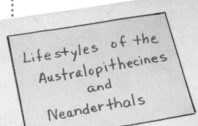

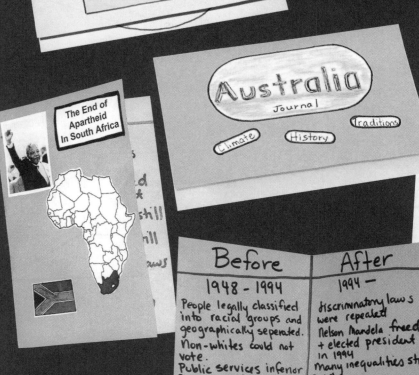

Folded Book

1. Make a *half-book*.

2. Fold it in half again like a *hamburger*. This makes a ready-made cover, and two small pages for information on the inside.

Use photocopied work sheets, Internet print outs, and student-drawn diagrams or maps to make this book. One sheet of paper becomes two activities and two grades.

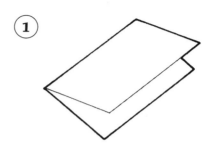

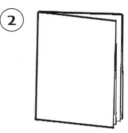

When folded, the worksheet becomes a book for recording notes and questions

Three-Quarter Book

1. Take a *two-tab* book and raise the left-hand tab.

2. Cut the tab off at the top fold line.

3. A larger book of information can be made by gluing several *three-quarter books* side-by-side.

Sketch or glue a graphic to the left, write one or more questions on the right, and record answers and information under the right tab.

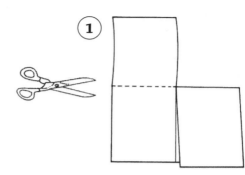

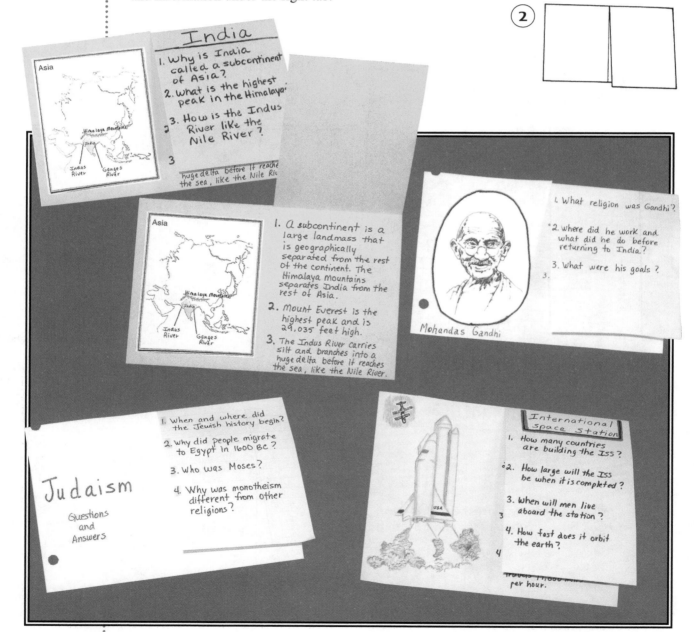

Bound Book

1. Take two sheets of paper (8 1/2" χ 11") and separately fold them like a *hamburger*. Place the papers on top of each other, leaving one sixteenth of an inch between the *mountain tops*.

2. Mark both folds one inch from the outer edges.

3. On one of the folded sheets, cut from the top and bottom edge to the marked spot on both sides.

4. On the second folded sheet, start at one of the marked spots and cut the fold between the two marks.

5. Take the cut sheet from step 3 and fold it like a *burrito*. Place the *burrito* through the other sheet and then open the *burrito*. Fold the bound pages in half to form an eight-page book.

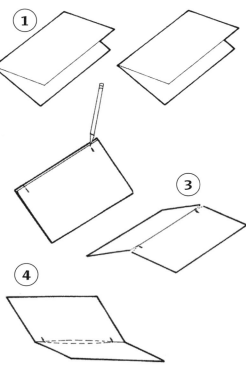

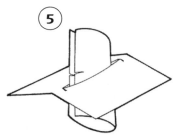

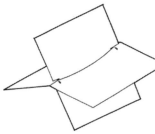

Picture-Frame Book

1. Fold a sheet of paper (8 1/2" χ 11") in half like a *hamburger*.

2. Open the *hamburger* and gently roll one side of the *hamburger* toward the *valley*. Try not to crease the roll.

3. Cut a rectangle out of the middle of the rolled side of the paper leaving a half-inch border, forming a frame.

4. Fold another sheet of paper (8 1/2" χ 11") in half like a *hamburger*. Apply glue to the inside border of the picture frame and place the folded, uncut sheet of paper inside.

Use this book to feature a person, place, or thing. Inside the picture frames, glue photographs, magazine pictures, computer-generated graphs, or have students sketch pictures. This book has three inside pages for writing and recording notes.

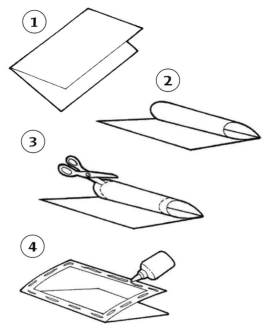

Two-Tab Book

1. Take a *folded book* and cut up the *valley* of the inside fold toward the *mountain top*. This cut forms two large tabs that can be used front and back for writing and illustrations.

2. The book can be expanded by making several of these folds and gluing them side-by-side.

Use this book with data occurring in twos. For example, use it for comparing and contrasting, determining cause and effect, finding similarities and differences, and more.

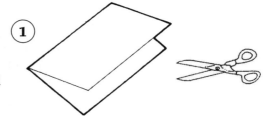

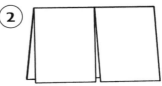

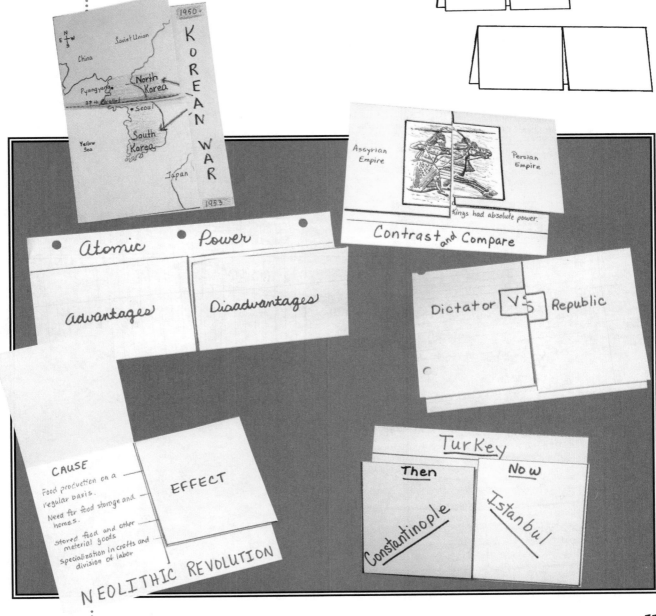

Pocket Book

1. Fold a sheet of paper (8 1/2" χ 11") in half like a *hamburger*.

2. Open the folded paper and fold one of the long sides up two inches to form a pocket. Refold along the *hamburger* fold so that the newly formed pockets are on the inside.

3. Glue the outer edges of the two-inch fold with a small amount of glue.

4. **Optional:** Glue a cover around the *pocket book.*

   Variation: Make a multi-paged booklet by gluing several pockets side-by-side. Glue a cover around the multi-paged *pocket book.*

Use 3" χ 5" index cards and quarter-sheets of notebook paper inside the pockets. Store student-made books, such as two-tab books and folded books in the pockets.

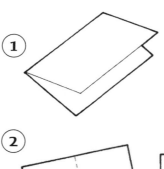

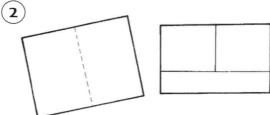

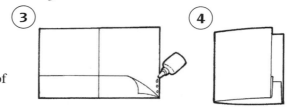

Matchbook

1. Fold a sheet of paper (8 1/2" χ 11") like a *hamburger,* but fold it so that one side is one inch longer than the other side.

2. Fold the one-inch tab over the short side forming an envelopelike fold.

3. Cut the front flap in half toward the *mountain top* to create two flaps.

Use this book to report on one thing, such as one person, place, or thing, or for reporting on two things, such as the cause and effect of the U.S. Monroe Doctrine.
Matchbooks can become interactive bulletin boards.

①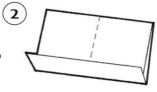

②

③

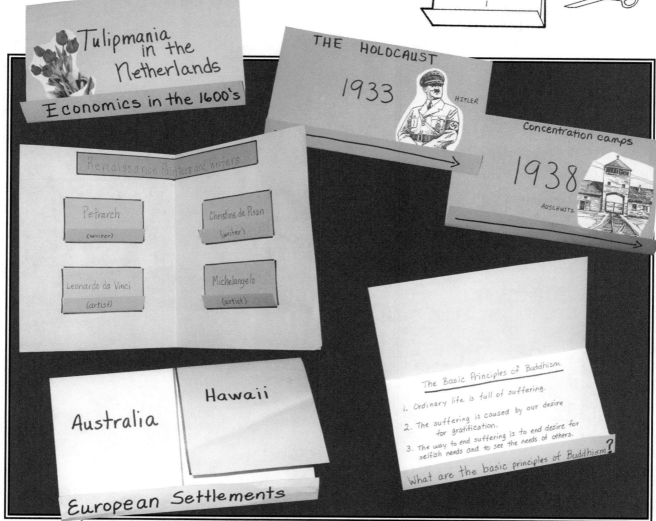

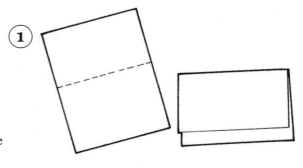

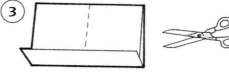

Shutter Fold

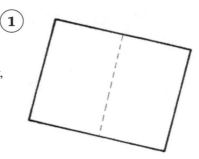

1. Begin as if you were going to make a *hamburger* but instead of creasing the paper, pinch it to show the midpoint.

2. Fold the outer edges of the paper to meet at the pinch, or mid-point, forming a *shutter fold.*

Use this book for data occurring in twos. Or, make this fold using 11" χ 17" paper and smaller books—such as the half book, journal, and two-tab book—can be glued inside to create a large project full of student work.

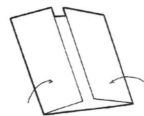

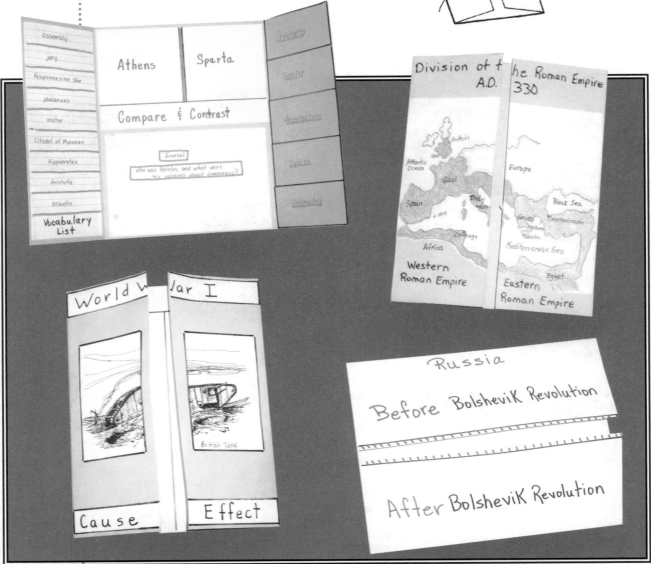

Forward-Backward Book

1. Stack three or more sheets of paper. On the top sheet trace a large circle.

2. With the papers still stacked, cut out the circles.

3. Staple the paper circles together along the left-hand side to create a book.

4. Label the cover and takes notes on the pages that open to the right.

5. Turn the book upside down and label the back. Takes notes on the pages that open to the right.

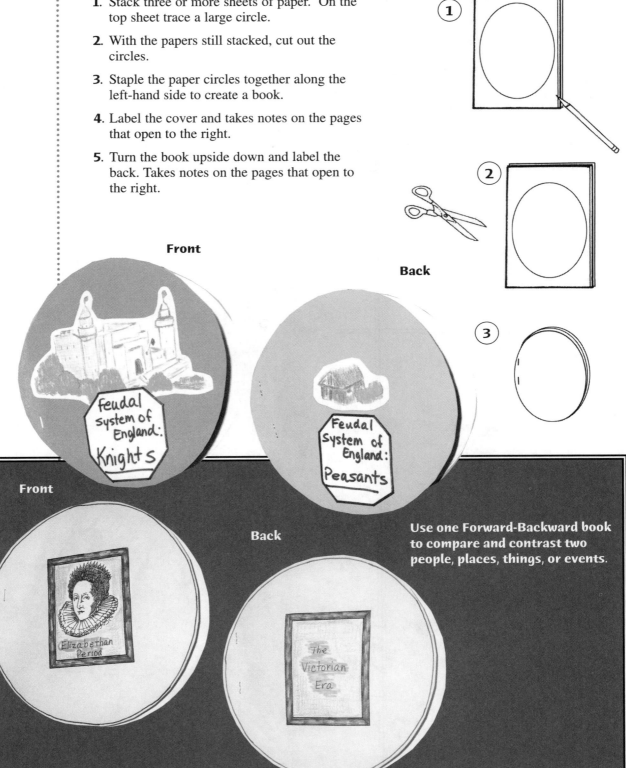

Front

Back

Feudal system of England: Knights

Feudal System of England: Peasants

Front

Back

Elizabethan Period

The Victorian Era

Use one Forward-Backward book to compare and contrast two people, places, things, or events.

Three-Tab Book

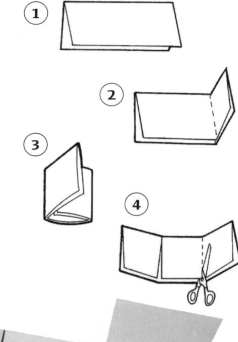

1. Fold a sheet of paper like a *hot dog*.

2. With the paper horizontal, and the fold of the *hot dog* up, fold the right side toward the center, trying to cover one half of the paper.

   NOTE: *If you fold the right edge over first, the final graphic organizer will open and close like a book.*

3. Fold the left side over the right side to make a book with three folds.

4. Open the folded book. Place your hands between the two thicknesses of paper and cut up the two *valleys* on one side only. This will form three tabs.

Use this book for data occurring in threes, and for two-part Venn diagrams.

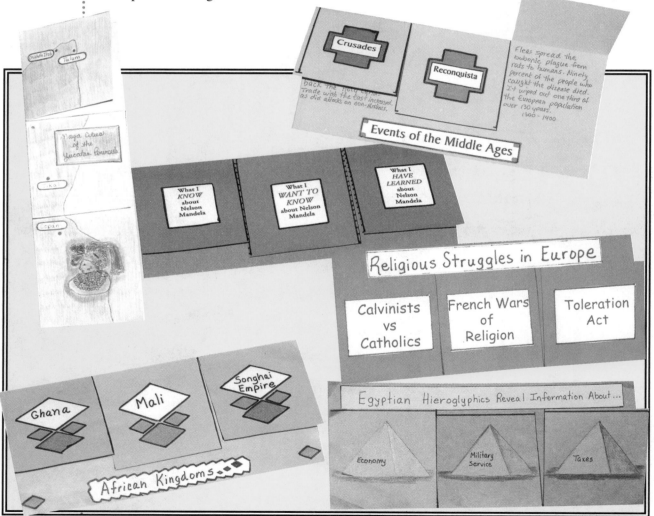

Three-Tab Book Variations

VARIATION A:
Draw overlapping circles on the three tabs to make a Venn Diagram

VARIATION B:
Cut each of the three tabs in half to make a six-tab book.

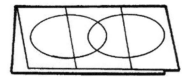

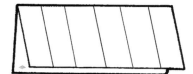

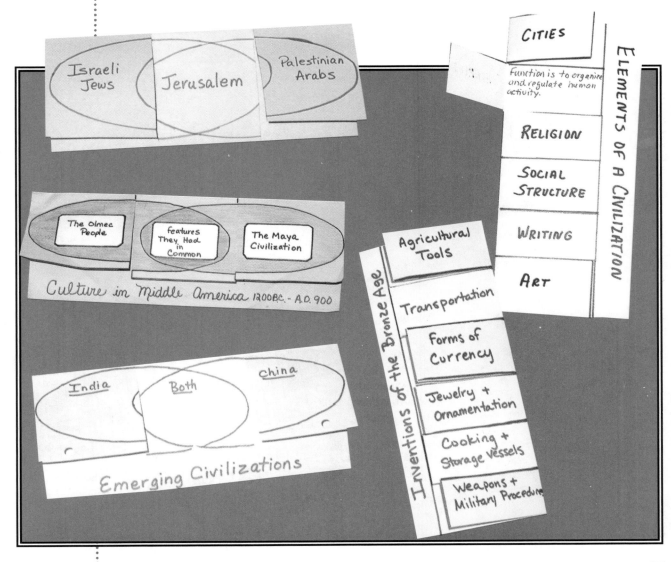

Pyramid Fold

1. Fold a sheet of paper (8 1/2" χ 11") into a *taco,* forming a square. Cut off the excess rectangular tab formed by the fold.

2. Open the folded *taco* and refold it the opposite way forming another *taco* and an X-fold pattern.

3. Cut one of the folds to the center of the X, or the midpoint, and stop. This forms two triangular-shaped flaps.

4. Glue one of the flaps under the other, forming a *pyramid.*

5. Label front sections and write information, notes, thoughts, and questions inside the pyramid on the back of the appropriate tab.

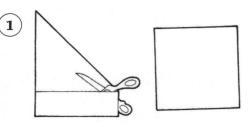

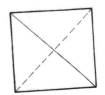

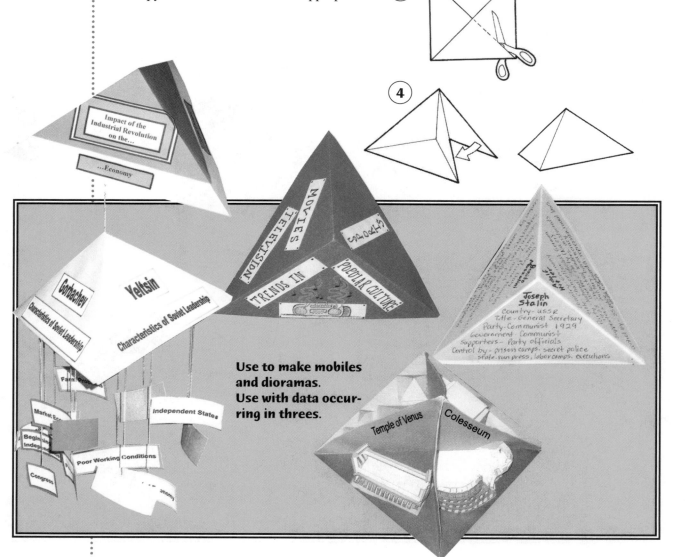

Use to make mobiles and dioramas.
Use with data occurring in threes.

Trifold Book

1. Fold a sheet of paper (8 1/2" χ 11") into thirds.

2. Use this book as is, or cut into shapes. If the trifold is cut, leave plenty of fold on both sides of the designed shape, so the book will open and close in three sections.

Use this book to make charts with three columns or rows, large Venn diagrams, reports on data occurring in threes, or to show the outside and inside of something and to write about it.

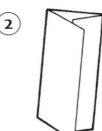

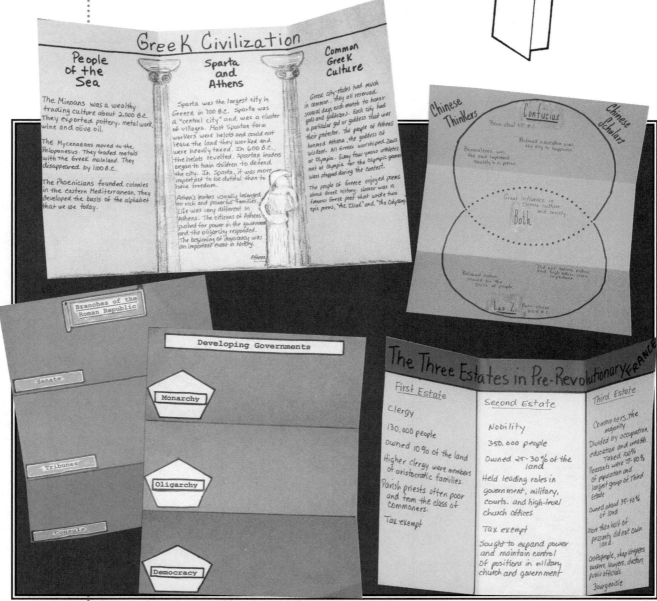

Three Pocket Book

1. Fold a horizontal sheet of paper (11" χ 17") into thirds.

2. Fold the bottom edge up two inches and crease well. Glue the outer edges of the two inch tab to create three pockets.

3. Label each pocket. Use to hold notes taken on index cards or quarter sheets of paper

Quarter sheets of notebook paper, or 3"x3" index cards can be used for notetaking activities.

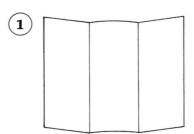

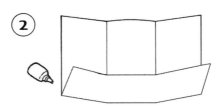

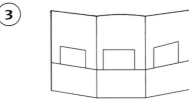

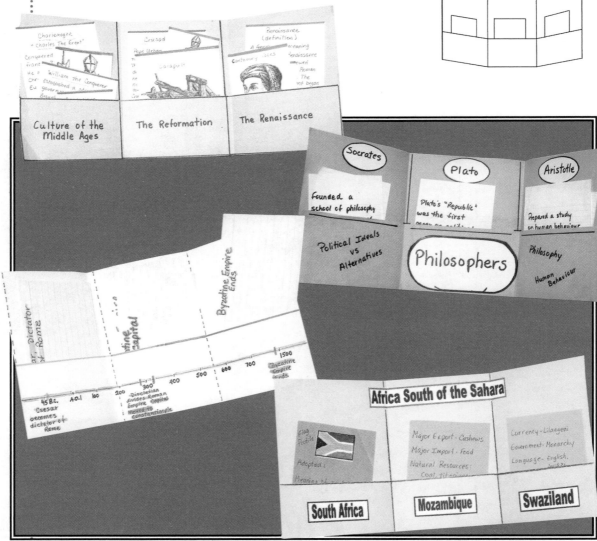

Four-Tab Book

1. Fold a sheet of paper (8 1/2" χ 11") in half like a *hot dog*.

2. Fold this long rectangle in half like a *hamburger*.

3. Fold both ends back to touch the *mountain top* or fold it like an *accordion*.

4. On the side with two *valleys* and one *mountain top*, make vertical cuts through one thickness of paper, forming four tabs.

Use this book for data occurring in fours. For example: the Four Noble Truths of Buddhism.

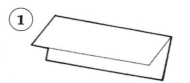

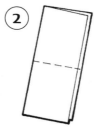
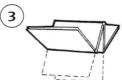

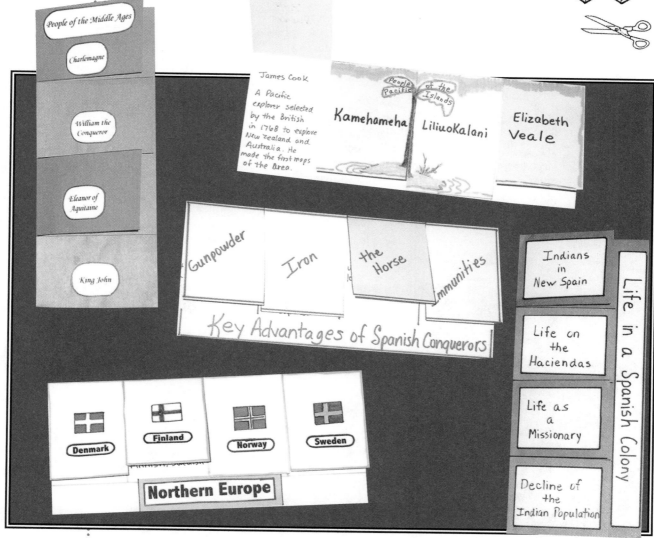

Standing Cube

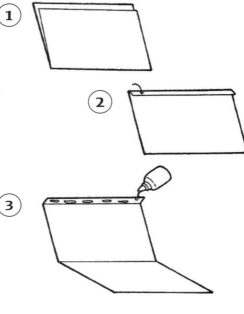

1. Use two sheets of the same size paper. Fold each like a *hamburger*. However, fold one side one half inch shorter than the other side. This will make a tab that extends out one half inch on one side.

2. Fold the long side over the short side of both sheets of paper, making tabs.

3. On one of the folded papers, place a small amount of glue along the the small folded tab, next to the *valley* but not in it.

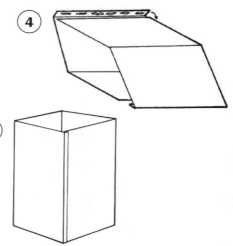

4. Place the non-folded edge of the second sheet of paper square into the *valley* and fold the glue-covered tab over this sheet of paper. Press flat until the glue holds. Repeat with the other side.

5. Allow the glue to dry completely before continuing. After the glue has dried, the cube can be collapsed flat to allow students to work at their desks. The cube can also be folded into fourths for easier storage, or for moving it to a display area.

Use with data occurring in fours or make it into a project. Make a small display cube using 8 1/2" χ 11" paper. Use 11" χ 17" paper to make large project cubes that you can glue other books onto for display. Notebook paper, photocopied sheets, magazine pictures, and current events can also be displayed on the large cube.

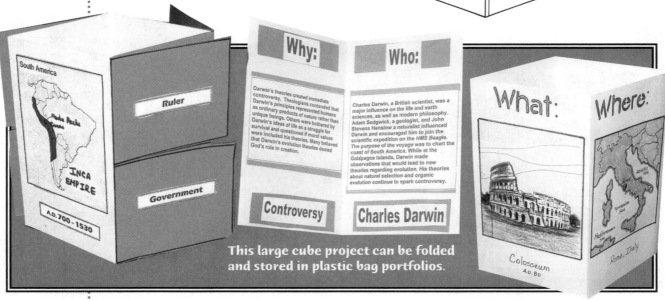

This large cube project can be folded and stored in plastic bag portfolios.

Four-Door Book

1. Make a *shutter fold* using 11" χ 17" or 12" χ 18" paper.

2. Fold the *shutter fold* in half like a *hamburger.* Crease well.

3. Open the project and cut along the two inside *valley* folds.

4. These cuts will form four doors on the inside of the project.

Use this fold for data occurring in fours. When folded in half like a *hamburger,* a finished *four-door book* can be glued inside a large (11" χ 17") *shutter fold* as part of a larger project.

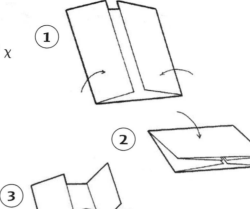

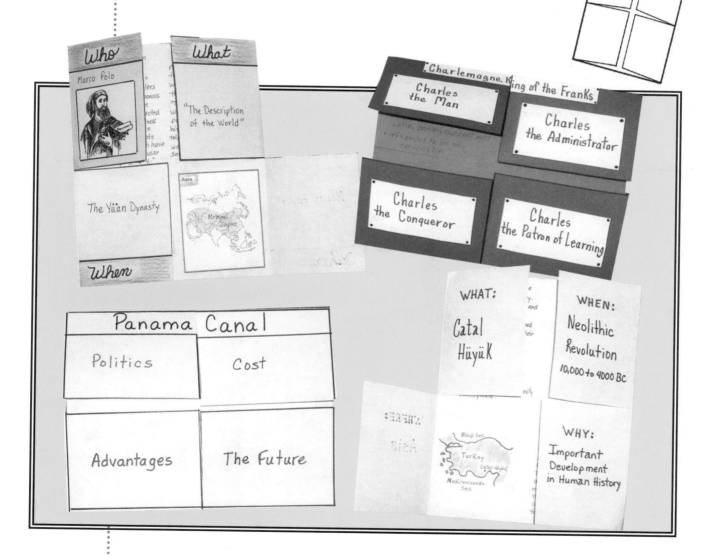

Envelope Fold

1. Fold a sheet of paper (8 1/2" χ 11") into a taco forming a square. Cut off the excess paper strip formed by the square.

2. Open the folded taco and refold it the opposite way forming another taco and an X fold pattern.

3. Open the taco fold and fold the corners toward the center point of the X forming a small square.

4. Trace this square on another sheet of paper. Cut and glue it to the inside of the envelope. Pictures can be placed under or on top of the tabs, or can be used to teach fractional parts.

Use this book for data occurring in fours. For example: the what, when, where, why of the Cold War.

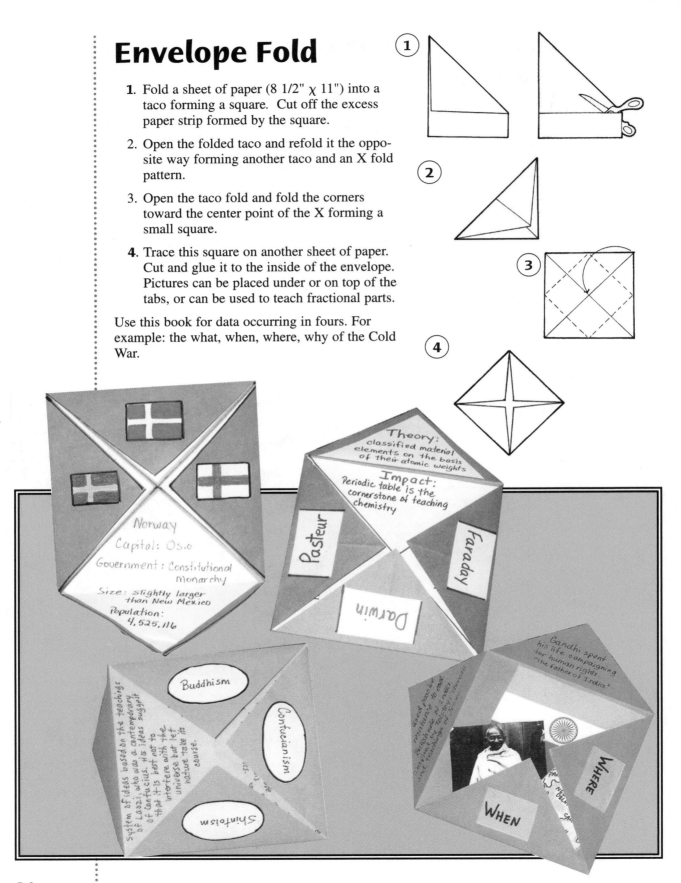

Layered-Look Book

1. Stack two sheets of paper (8 1/2" χ 11") so that the back sheet is one inch higher than the front sheet.

2. Bring the bottom of both sheets upward and align the edges so that all of the layers or tabs are the same distance apart.

3. When all tabs are an equal distance apart, fold the papers and crease well.

4. Open the papers and glue them together along the *valley* or inner center fold or, staple them along the mountain.

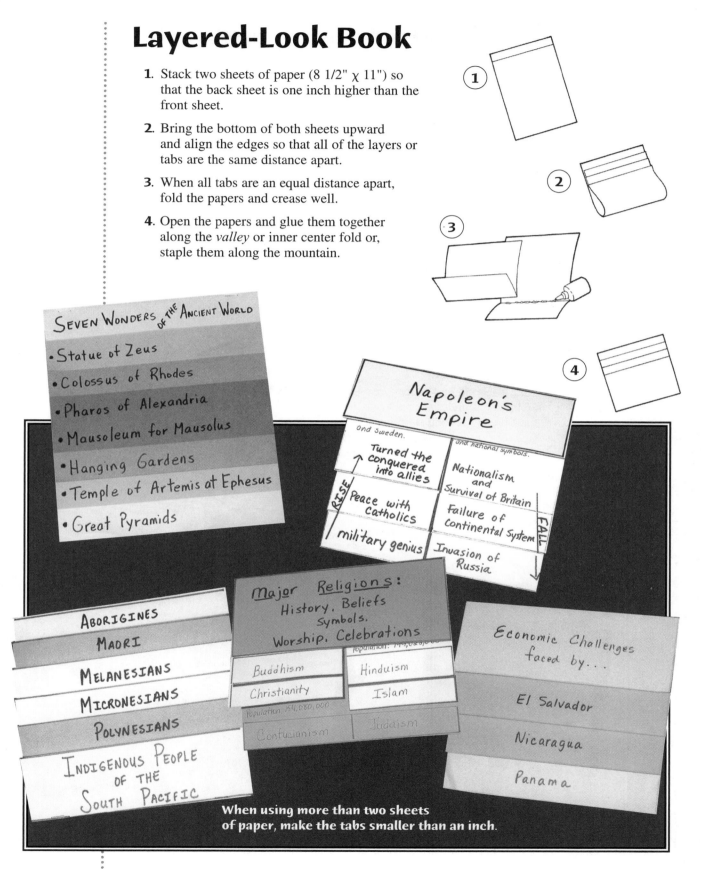

SEVEN WONDERS OF THE ANCIENT WORLD

• Statue of Zeus
• Colossus of Rhodes
• Pharos of Alexandria
• Mausoleum for Mausolus
• Hanging Gardens
• Temple of Artemis at Ephesus
• Great Pyramids

Napoleon's Empire

and sweden.
and national symbols.
RISE
Turned the conquered into allies
Nationalism and Survival of Britain
Peace with Catholics
Failure of Continental System
FALL
military genius
Invasion of Russia

ABORIGINES
MAORI
MELANESIANS
MICRONESIANS
POLYNESIANS
INDIGENOUS PEOPLE OF THE SOUTH PACIFIC

Major Religions:
History. Beliefs
Symbols.
Worship. Celebrations

Population: 14,080,000

Buddhism   Hinduism
Christianity   Islam

Population: 154,080,000

Confucianism   Judaism

Economic Challenges faced by...

El Salvador

Nicaragua

Panama

When using more than two sheets of paper, make the tabs smaller than an inch.

Top-Tab Book

1. Fold a sheet of paper (8 1/2" χ 11") in half like a *hamburger.* Cut the center fold, forming two half sheets.

2. Fold one of the half sheets four times. Begin by folding in half like a *hamburger,* fold again like a *hamburger,* and finally again like a *hamburger.* This folding has formed your pattern of four rows and four columns, or 16 small squares.

3. Fold two sheets of paper (8 1/2" χ 11") in half like a *hamburger.* Cut the center folds, forming four half sheets.

4. Hold the pattern vertically and place on a half sheet of paper under the pattern. Cut the bottom right hand square out of both sheets. Set this first page aside.

5. Take a second half sheet of paper and place it under the pattern. Cut the first and second right hand squares out of both sheets. Place the second page on top of the first page.

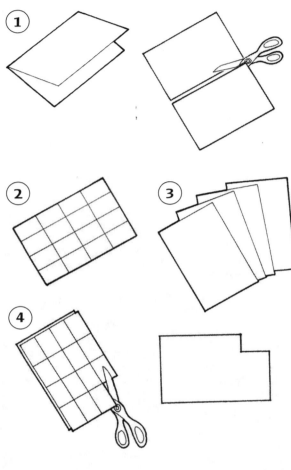

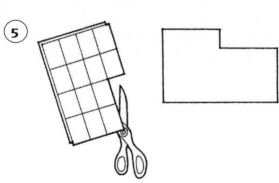

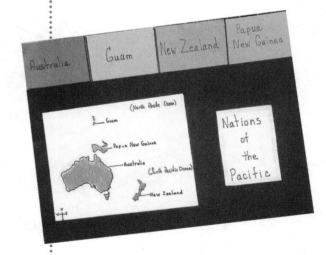

6. Take a third half sheet of paper and place it under the pattern. Cut the first, second, and third right hand squares out of both sheets. Place this third page on top of the second page.

7. Place the fourth, uncut half sheet of paper behind the three cut out sheets, leaving four aligned tabs across the top of the book. Staple several times on the left side. You can also place glue along the left paper edges, and stack them together. The glued spine is very strong.

8. Cut a final half sheet of paper with no tabs and staple along the left side to form a cover.

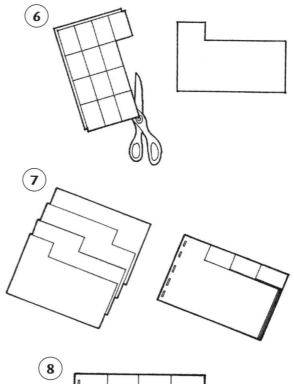

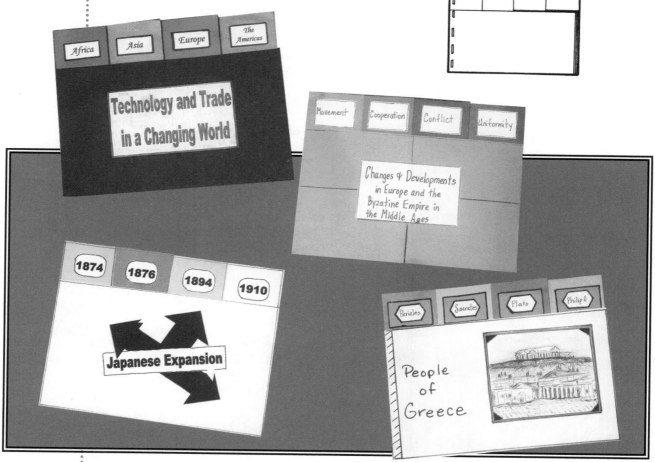

Accordion Book

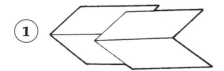

NOTE: *Steps 1 and 2 should be done only if paper is too large to begin with.*

1. Fold the selected paper into *hamburgers*.

2. Cut the paper in half along the fold lines.

3. Fold each section of paper into *hamburgers*. However, fold one side one half inch shorter than the other side. This will form a tab that is one half inch long.

4. Fold this tab forward over the shorter side, and then fold it back away from the shorter piece of paper (in other words, fold it the opposite way).

5. Glue together to form an *accordion* by gluing a straight edge of one section into the *valley* of another section.

NOTE: *Stand the sections on end to form an accordion to help students visualize how to glue them together. (See illustration.)*

Always place the extra tab at the back of the book so you can add more pages later.

Use this book for timelines, student projects that grow, sequencing events or data, and biographies.

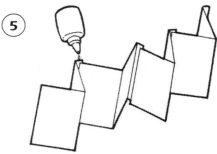

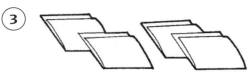

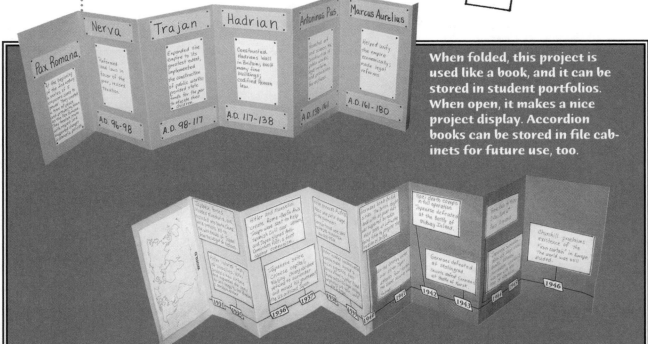

When folded, this project is used like a book, and it can be stored in student portfolios. When open, it makes a nice project display. Accordion books can be stored in file cabinets for future use, too.

Pop-Up Book

1. Fold a sheet of paper (8 1/2" χ 11") in half like a *hamburger*.

2. Beginning at the fold, or *mountain* top, cut one or more tabs.

3. Fold the tabs back and forth several times until there is a good fold line formed.

4. Partially open the *hamburger* fold and push the tabs through to the inside.

5. With one small dot of glue, glue figures for the *pop-up book* to the front of each tab. Allow the glue to dry before going on to the next step.

6. Make a cover for the book by folding another sheet of paper in half like a *hamburger*. Place glue around the outside edges of the *pop-up book* and firmly press inside the *hamburger* cover.

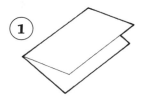

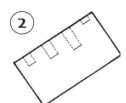

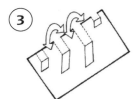

Pop-up sheets can be glued side-by-side to make pop-up books.

Women Gained the Right to Vote

1980 Iraq

1945 Italy and Japan

1920 United States of America

1893 New Zealand

WORLD

The Right to Vote ✓

The Titanic

A luxury sailing vessel, the Titanic was built in Ireland. It sailed from Southampton, England on its maiden voyage with more than 2200 passengers and crew. While speeding towards New York City, the ship received six ice warnings. It struck an iceberg off the coast of Newfoundland on April 14, 1912. The Titanic sank in less than three hours. There were lifeboats for approximately half of the passengers. More than 1500 of the 2200 passengers died. The 705 survivors were rescued by another ship.

Folding into Fifths

1. Fold a sheet of paper in half like a hotdog or hamburger for a five tab book, or leave open for a folded table or chart.

2. Fold the paper so that one third is exposed and two thirds are covered.

3. Fold the two thirds section in half.

4. Fold the one third section (single thickness) backward to form a fold line.

The paper will be divided into fifths when opened

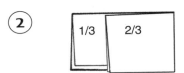

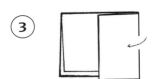

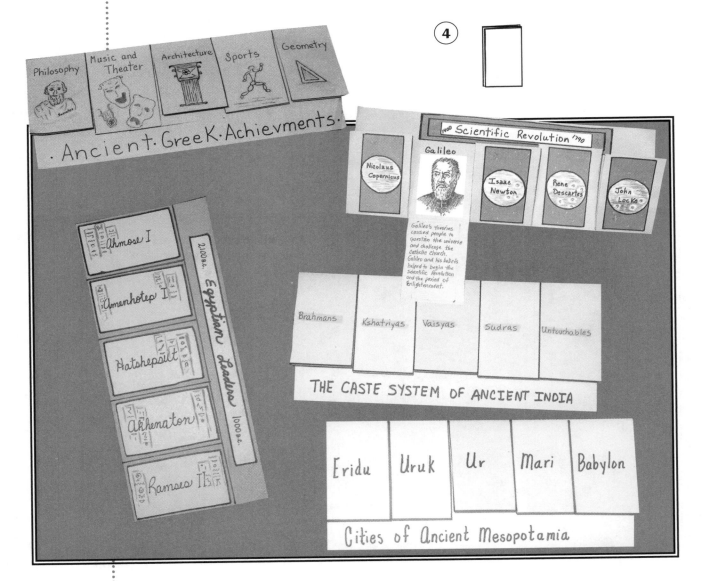

Folded Table or Chart

1. Fold the number of vertical columns needed to make the table or chart.

2. Fold the horizontal rows needed to make the table or chart.

3. Label the rows and columns.

Remember: Tables are organized along vertical and horizontal axes, while charts are organized along one axis, either horizontal or vertical.

Table

Chart

India	Mauryan Empire	Gupta Empire
Dates	324-301 BC	A.D. 320-late 5th century
Government	Kings centralized government Provinces ruled by governors	Kings
Economy	Expanded regional trade Major crossroads of large commercial network	Prosperous trade with china, Southeast Asia and Mediterranean Sea region

Monarch/ Country	Achievments
William of Normandy King of England	First census of Europe since Roman times Developed tax system
Henry II of England 1154-1189	Strengthened the royal courts
King John of England	Signed the Magna Carta
Edward I of England	Development of English Parliment
Phillip II Augustus of France 1180-1223	Regained territory from the English
Louis IX of France	"Greatest" medieval French King Made a saint by Catholic church brought justice to his people

Early Civilizations in Mesoamerica	People	Location	Religion	Decline
Aztec	Monarch, commoner indentured workers. farmers, slaves, captives;women allowed to own property + became priests	Valley of Mexico and central Mexico Capital city was Tenochtitlan	Based on belief of good and evil struggling in the universe Practiced human sacrifice	Hernán Corte's arrived in 1519 Aztecs without immunity to disease died. Fighting with soldiers.
Mayan	Rulers claimed to be descended from the gods. Nobles, Scribes, priests Artists, officials merchants,commoners slaves, farmers	Yucatán Peninsula.	Believed all of life was controlled by divine powers Human sacrifices of prisoners captured in battle	Possible invasion internal revolt natural disaster reduced crop production
Olmec	Lowlands along Gulf of Mexico south of Veracruz was a busy trade center. farming area.	Gulf of Mexico coast line	Built large cities that were Centers for religious rituals. Built pyramids, carved stone figures	400 BC.
Toltec	warriors	Center of Toltec at Tula, in present-day Mexico City Conquests in Mayan lands of Guatemala and Yucatan	Builders of Pyramids and palaces.	A.D. 1200

Folding a Circle into Tenths

1. Fold a paper circle in half.

2. Fold the half circle so that one third is exposed and two thirds are covered.

3. Fold the one third (single thickness) backward to form a fold line.

4. Fold the two thirds section in half.

5. The half circle will be divided into fifths. When opened, the circle will be divided into tenths.

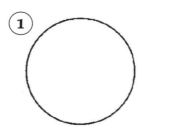

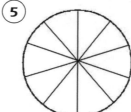

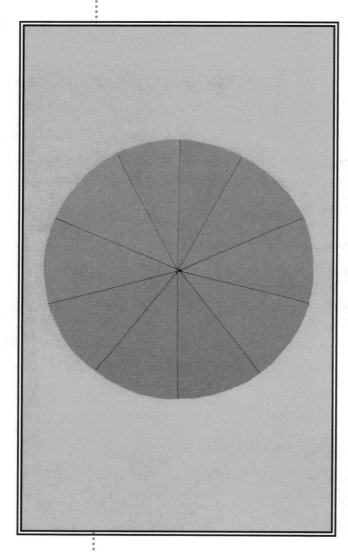

NOTE: *Paper squares and rectangles are folded into tenths the same way. Fold them so that one third is exposed and two thirds is covered. Continue with steps 3 and 4.*

Circle Graph

1. Cut out two circles using a pattern.

2. Fold one of the circles in half on each axis, forming fourths. Cut along one of the fold lines (the radius) to the middle of each circle. Flatten the circle.

3. Slip the two circles together along the cuts until they overlap completely.

4. Spin one of the circles while holding the other stationary. Estimate how much of each of the two (or you can add more) circles should be exposed to illustrate given percentages or fractional parts of data. Add circles to represent more than two percentages.

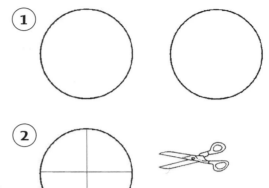

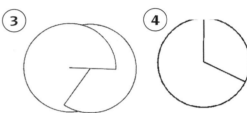

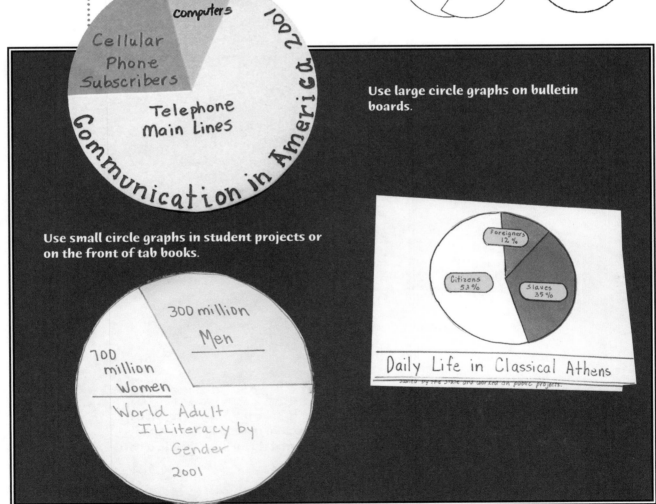

Use large circle graphs on bulletin boards.

Use small circle graphs in student projects or on the front of tab books.

Vocabulary Book

1. Fold a sheet of notebook paper in half like a *hotdog*.

2. On one side, cut every third line. This results in ten tabs on wide ruled notebook paper and twelve tabs on college ruled.

3. Label the tabs.

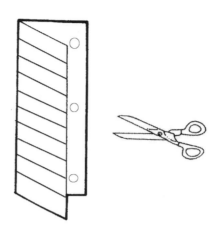

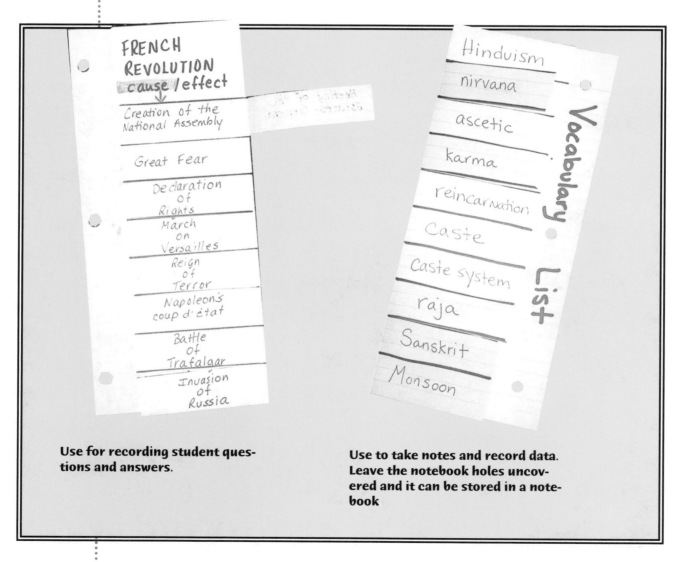

FRENCH
REVOLUTION
cause/effect
↓
Creation of the
National Assembly

Great Fear

Declaration
Of
Rights

March
On
Versailles

Reign
Of
Terror

Napoleon's
coup d'état

Battle
Of
Trafalgar

Invasion
Of
Russia

Hinduism

nirvana

ascetic

karma

reincarnation

caste

Caste system

raja

Sanskrit

Monsoon

Vocabulary List

Use for recording student questions and answers.

Use to take notes and record data. Leave the notebook holes uncovered and it can be stored in a notebook

Concept-Map Book

1. Fold a sheet of paper along the long or short axis, leaving a two-inch tab uncovered along the top.

2. Fold in half or in thirds.

3. Unfold and cut along the two or three inside fold lines.

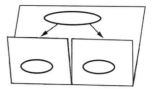

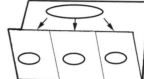

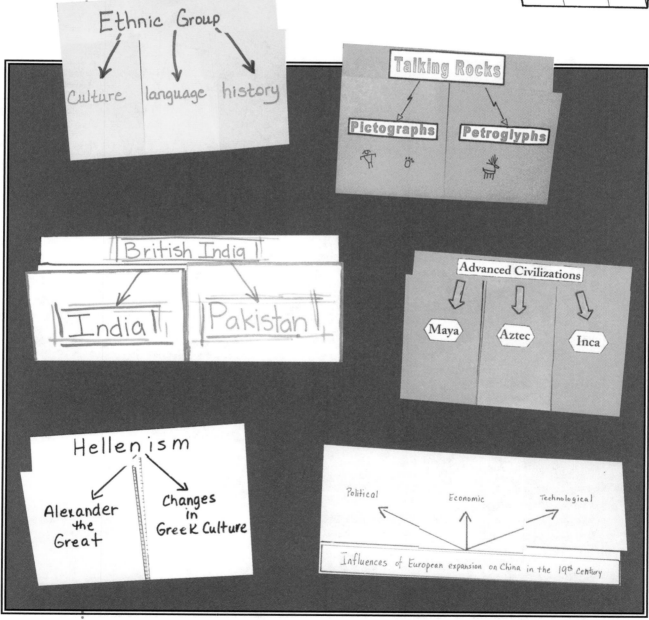

Four-Door Diorama

1. Make a *four-door book* out of a *shutter fold*.

2. Fold the two inside corners back to the outer edges (*mountains*) of the *shutter fold*. This will result in two *tacos* that will make the *four-door book* look like it has a shirt collar. Do the same thing to the bottom of the *four-door book*. When finished, four small triangular *tacos* have been made.

3. Form a 90-degree angle and overlap the folded triangles to make a display case that doesn't use staples or glue. (It can be collapsed for storage.)

4. Or, as illustrated, cut off all four triangles, or *tacos*. Staple or glue the sides.

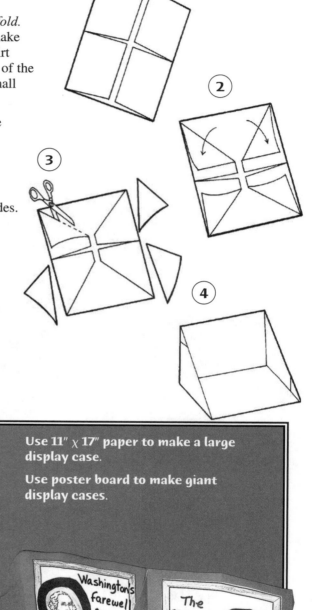

Use 11″ χ 17″ paper to make a large display case.

Use poster board to make giant display cases.

Glue display cases end-to-end to compare and contrast or to sequence events or data.

Display Case

1. Make a *taco* fold and cut off the rectangular tab formed. This will result in a square.

2. Fold the square into a *shutter fold.*

3. Unfold and fold the square into another *shutter fold* perpendicular to the direction of the first. This will form a small square at each of the four corners of the sheet of paper.

4. As illustrated, cut along two fold lines on opposite sides of the large square.

5. Collapse in and glue the cut tabs to form an open box.

How to Make a Lid

Fold another open-sided box using a square of paper one half inch larger than the square used to make the first box. This will make a lid that fits snugly over the display box. *Example:* If the base is made out of an 8 1/2" paper square, then make the top out of a 9" square.

Cut a hole out of the lid and cover the opening with a cut piece of acetate used on overhead projectors. Heavy, clear plastic wrap or scraps from a laminating machine also will work. Secure the clear plastic sheet to the inside of the lid with glue or tape.

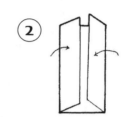

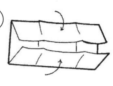
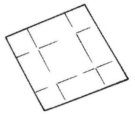
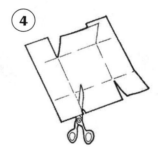

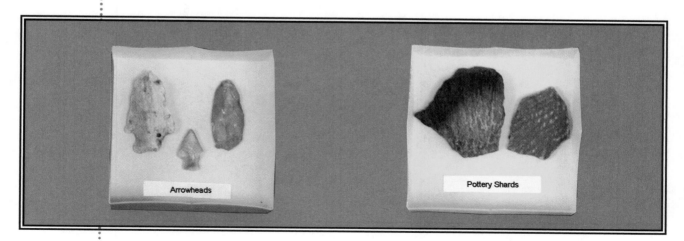

Arrowheads

Pottery Shards

Project Board with Tabs

1. Draw a large illustration or a series of small illustrations or write on the front of one of the pieces of selected-size paper.

2. Pinch and slightly fold the paper at the point where a tab is desired on the illustrated project board. Cut into the paper on the fold. Cut straight in, then cut up to form an "L." When the paper is unfolded, it will form a tab with an illustration on the front.

3. After all tabs have been cut, glue this front sheet onto a second piece of paper. Place glue around all four edges and in the middle, away from tabs.

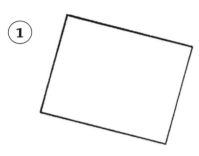

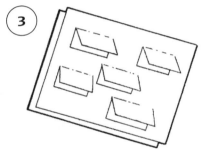

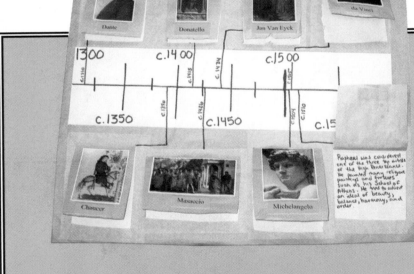

Students write or draw under the tabs. If the project is made as a bulletin board using butcher paper, quarter and half-sheets of paper can be glued under the tabs.

Billboard Project

1. Fold all pieces of the same size of paper in half like *hamburgers*.

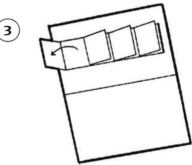

2. Place a line of glue at the top and bottom of one side of each folded billboard section and glue them edge-to-edge on a background paper or project board. If glued correctly, all doors will open from right to left.

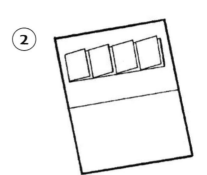

3. Pictures, dates, words, etc., go on the front of each billboard section. When opened, writing or drawings can be seen on the inside left of each section. The base, or the part glued to the background, is perfect for more in-depth information or definitions.

Use for timelines or sequencing data, such as the key events of WWII

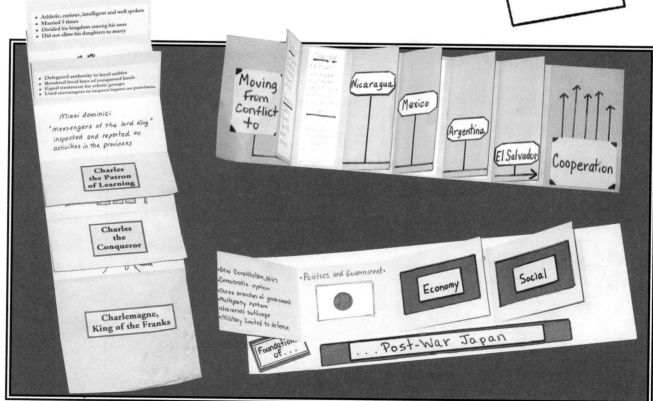

Sentence Strips

1. Take two sheets of paper (8 1/2" x 11") and fold into hamburgers. Cut along the fold lines making four half sheets. *(Use as many half sheets as necessary for additional pages to your book.)*

2. Fold each sheet in half like a hotdog.

3. Place the folds side-by-side and staple them together on the left side.

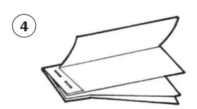

4. 1" from the stapled edge, cut the front page of each folded section up to the mountain top. These cuts form flaps that can be raised and lowered.

To make a half-cover, use a sheet of colored paper cut one inch longer than the book. Glue the back of the last sheet to the construction paper strip leaving one inch, on the left side, to fold over and cover the original staples. Staple or glue this half-cover in place.

Sentence-Strip Holder

1. Fold a sheet of paper (8 1/2" χ 11") in half like a *hamburger*.

2. Open the *hamburger* and fold the two outer edges toward the *valley*. This forms a *shutter fold*.

3. Fold one of the inside edges of the shutter back to the outside fold. This fold forms a floppy "L."

4. Glue the floppy L-tab down to the base so that it forms a strong, straight L-tab.

5. Glue the other shutter side to the front of this L-tab. This forms a tent that is the backboard for the flashcards or student work to be displayed.

6. Fold the edge of the L-tab up one quarter to one half to form a lip that will keep the student work from slipping off the holder.

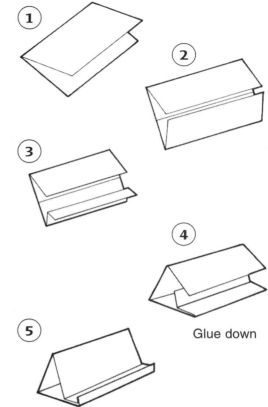

Glue down

Use holders to display student work on a table, or glue onto a bulletin board to make it interactive.

World History Activities
Using
Foldables

General Topics

The following World History topics are covered in this section.

The Stone Age

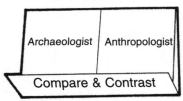

Archaeologist | Anthropologist
Compare & Contrast

Two-tab matchbook

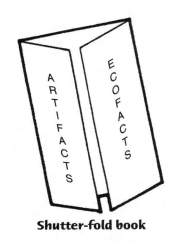

A R T I F A C T S | E C O F A C T S

Shutter-fold book

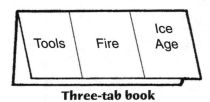

Tools | Fire | Ice Age

Three-tab book

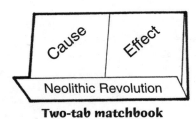

Cause | Effect
Neolithic Revolution

Two-tab matchbook

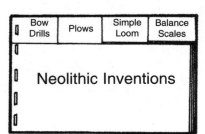

Bow Drills | Plows | Simple Loom | Balance Scales
Neolithic Inventions

Top-tab book

Skill	Activity Suggestion	Foldable Parts
define	paleolithic	1
compare and contrast	archaeologists and anthropologists	2
search the web	for information on the Stone Age: • Paleolithic Age, also called the Old Stone Age • Neolithic Age also called the New Stone Age	2
make a chart	listing items an archaeologist might find from these Ages and describe the information they could impart	2
differentiate between	artifacts and ecofacts	2
research and compare	two methods scientists use to date artifacts and fossils: • radiocarbon dating • dendrochronology • thermoluminescence • potassium-argon method	2
report on	the use of DNA in discovering clues to the past	1
describe	three factors that shaped the Old Stone Age • development of tools • use of fire • the Ice Age	3
explain	how the Ice Age might have affected population movements and map possible migration routes	2
describe	three ways the use of fire changed human lifestyle: • warmth • protection • cooking	3
	three ways in which early people changed the world around them by their daily actions, and compare these changes to those made by humans today	3
speculate	on the significance of Neanderthals burying their dead	1
show cause and effect	of the Neolithic Revolution	2
make a table	of crops and animals raised on each continent during the New Stone Age	any number
list	four important inventions of the New Stone Age	4
define	civilization: include information on the importance of cities, communication, government, religion, social structure, transportation	6
investigate	the what, where, when, why of the following: • of the Neolithic Revolution, Catal Hüyük • cave paintings in Altamira, Spain • cave paintings in Lascaux, France	4
investigate	the who, what, when, where of the following: • Louis Bazet Seymore Leakey and Mary N. Leakey • Donald Carl Johanson	4
explain	the significance of the copper tools found with the mummified Iceman of the Alps, nicknamed Ötzi	1
compare	ancient and recent megalithic monuments and structures For example: Stonehenge in England (ancient) and the megaliths of Easter Island (recent)	2
make a timeline	of artifact discoveries that illustrate the early history of stone tools and weapons	any number
	of the history of the domestication of animals	any number

Copper, Bronze, and Iron Ages

Skill	Activity Suggestion	Foldable Parts
define	metallurgy	1
explain	why chronologically, terms such as Copper Age, Bronze Age, and Iron Age have limited value (It is important to understand that the use of different metals took place at different times in different cultures.)	1
list and explain	three advantages to using metal over stone when producing tools and weapons	3
sequence	developments occurring during the Stone Age, Copper Age, the Bronze Age, and the Iron Age	4
compare and contrast	the first copper tools used to later bronze tools	2
make a time line	showing the use of bronze tools in different regions of the world: • 3000 BCE, Greece. • 1800 BCE, China • 1000 AD, pre-Columbian America	any number
investigate	the who, what, when, where of the Iceman of the Alps, nicknamed Ötzi, and his importance to our understanding of the Copper Age (about 4,000 to (2,200 B.C.E.)	4
Venn diagram	copper, tin, together make bronze	3
describe	how new inventions of the Bronze Age changed each of the following: • agricultural tools • transportation • forms of currency • jewelry making and ornamentation • cooking and storage vessels • weapons and military procedures	6
research	and report on three ways in which the use of iron changed life during the Iron Age	3
determine	why first interpretations of archaeological findings are not always accurate and compare and contrast the initial and final interpretations of when the Ice Man lived	2
	why burial sites are important to archaeologists and how they provide information on early cultures	2
discover	locations in Europe and the Americas where early cultures changed the shape of the Earth by moving large amounts of dirt or rock	2
	cultures of the Copper Age and cultures of the Iron Age	2
speculate	as to the importance of tin as a natural resource and the importance of tin as an item of trade before and after the discovery of bronze	2
investigate	the what, when, where of the 1984 excavation of an ancient shipwreck (13th-to 14th century) off the coast of Turkish at Uluburun led by American archaeologist George F. Bass	4
differentiate	between the three phases of the Bronze Age in the Middle East and the eastern Mediterranean—early, middle, and late	3

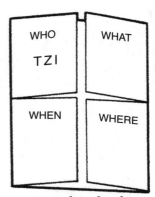

Four-door book

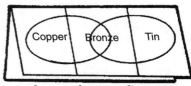

Three-tab Venn diagram

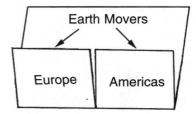

1x2 Chart

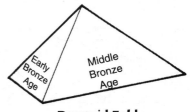

Two-tab concept map

Pyramid Fold

Mesopotamia

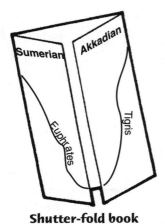

Shutter-fold book

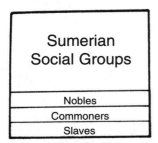

**Layer book
(2 sheets of paper)**

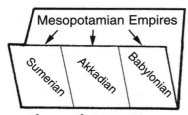

Three-tab concept map

Picture-frame book

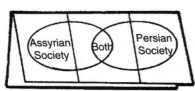

Three-tab Venn diagram

Skill	Activity Suggestion	Foldable Parts
compare	a map of ancient Mesopotamia to a current map of the same area, and explain how it got its name and why it is sometimes called *Fertile Crescent*	2
	two great civilizations that developed around rivers --Tigris and Euphrates, Nile, Indus, others	2
search the web	for information on a Neanderthal grave found in Shanidar Cave, Zagros Mountains, Iraq and analyze what it tells about early people in this area	2
describe	the land of the Fertile Crescent as desert, rocky mountains, and fertile river land	3
list	the three major social groups (nobles, commoners, slaves) of the Sumerian city-states and their duties	3
speculate	how trade might have led to the earliest writing	1
compare and contrast	cuneiform and hieroglyphics including the methods and materials used for each	2
explain	how floods of the Tigris and Euphrates affected the lives of the Mesopotamians and investigate their use of irrigation	2
report on	any five inventions during this Bronze Age civilization: • wheel • the plow • code of law • written language • architectural advances including the arch • base 60 number system, others	5
draw and label	a Sumerian city-state (walled city, land used for agriculture, ziggurat temple, royal palaces, and mud-brick houses and stores, and more)	any number
investigate	the who, what, when, and where of: • Sargon I of Akkad • Sargon II • Hammurabi, Babylonian King • Suleiman I, the Magnificent	4
	the what, where, when, why of: • the *Epic of Gilgamesh* • the *Code of Hammurabi*	4 4
Venn diagram	Tigris and Euphrates Rivers, Nile River, both	3
	Sumerian King, Egyptian Pharaoh, both	3
concept map	Mesopotamia and its three empires: • Sumerian • Akkadian • Babylonian	3
investigate	the city-states of Sumer before and after they were united under one ruler--Sargon	2
make a table of information	on the Sumerians, Babylonians, Assyrians, and the Israelites: record information on their writing, leaders, government/law, and their religion—monotheism or polytheism	any number
compare and contrast	the religious and cultural society of Babylonia with the warlike society of Assyria	2
describe	three military advantages of the Assyrians	3
research	the library of King Ashurbanipal located at Nineveh	1
compare and contrast	Babylon under the rule of Hammurabi and under the Chaldean rule of Nebuchadnezzar II	2
Venn diagram	Assyrian society, Persian society, and both	3
investigate	the what, where, when, why/how of: • the Hanging Gardens of Babylon • the Tower of Babel	4

Ancient Egypt

Skill	Activity Suggestion	Foldable Parts
compare and contrast	Upper Egypt and Lower Egypt	2
explain	three things the Nile River provided for Egyptian civilization:	3
	how the Egyptians viewed life and death and compare their views to views commonly held today	2
sequence	the steps of mummification	any number
Venn diagram	land of drought, land of flood, both	3
describe	how Egyptians utilized currents and the Etesian winds (northwest, summer winds) to develop two-way trade along the Nile	2
list	cities and important locations along the east bank and along the west bank of the Nile River and compare the two riverbanks	2
outline	the relationship between the annual Nile floods, the star Sirius, and the Egyptian calendar	3
speculate	how Egyptians farming lifestyle influenced their views on death	1
investigate	the who, what, when, where of: • Menes, first Pharaoh of Egypt • Imhotep, architect of first pyramid • Howard Carter, archaeologist and Egyptologist • Tutankhamun, Pharaoh,18th Dynasty • Hatshepsut, the first woman Pharaoh • King Akhenaton, the "heretic king" • the Ptolemys, Greek kings of Egypt (305-30 BC)	4
	the what, where, when, why/how of: • the Great Pyramid at Giza, last remaining Wonder of the Ancient World • Egyptian hieroglyphs and the Rosetta Stone • Valley of the Kings • the Sphinx • Egyptian *Book of the Dead* • the New Kingdom, 1532 BC	4
Venn diagram	Upper Egypt, Lower Egypt, both	3
describe	three types of tombs	3
	two ways Egyptians prepared for the afterlife	2
make a table	of four of Egypt's gods and goddesses and their symbolism, appearances, and myths	4
compare and contrast	classes of Egyptian society and their rights and responsibilities	any number
make a table	of key events, inventions, and leaders of the Old Kingdom, Middle Kingdom, and New Kingdom	3
list	three things the Pharaohs of Middle Kingdom did to make Egypt prosperous	3
show cause and effect	of Egypt becoming an Empire during the New Kingdom	2
compare and contrast	rights of women under the code of Hammurabi and rights of Egyptian women today	2
make a timeline	of the history of Ancient Egypt 3,500 B.C. to 1100 B.C.	any number
write	7 days of journal entries made by a laborer on the Great Pyramid at Giza	7

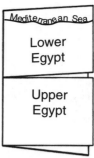

Two-tab book

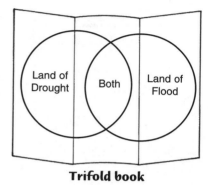

Trifold book

God/ Goddess	Symbolism	Appearance	Myths
Osiris			
Isis			
Thoth			

4x4 Folded chart

Three-tab book

Indus River Valley

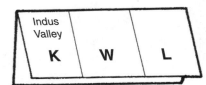

Three-tab book

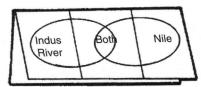

Three-tab Venn diagram

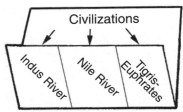

Three-tab concept map

Hindu Caste System
Brahman
Kshartriya
Vaishya
Shudra
Harijans

**Layer book
(3 sheets of paper)**

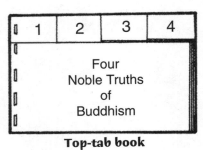

Top-tab book

Skill	Activity Suggestion	Foldable Parts
K-W-L	write about what you know, want to know, and what you learn about the Indus Valley civilizations	3
compare	a map of ancient Indus River Valley to a current map of the same area	2
outline	the history of farming including information on evidence of early farming in the Indus Valley, 6000 B.C.	any number
Venn diagram	Indus River, Nile River, both	3
compare and contrast	Indus River civilizations, Nile River civilizations, and Tigris-Euphrates River civilizations	3
report on	what is known and what is not known about the Harappan civilization of the ancient Indus Valley	2
speculate	as to what the discovery of ancient children's toys tells us about Indus Valley civilizations	any number
explain	why less is known about the Harappan civilization than other civilizations such as Sumerian	1
make a table	of trade routes and goods traded between the Indus River Valley and other ancient civilizations	1
identify	the Dravidians	1
describe	the Aryans, their history, and their migration route	3
trace	the origins of the Sanskrit language	1
research	how Hinduism grew out of the beliefs of the Aryans	1
outline	the caste system and its five classes: • Brahman (priests) • Kshatriya (warriors and rulers) • Vaishya (professionals and merchants) • Shudra (laborers) • Harijans ("untouchables")	5
define	reincarnation as a belief in a cycle of life-- birth, death, and rebirth	3
write	about the Four Noble Truths of Buddhism: 1. Life is filled with suffering. 2. Suffering is caused by people's wants. 3. Suffering can be ended if people quit wanting things. 4. To stop wanting things, people must follow eight basic laws.	4
make a concept map	Buddhism—founder, basic beliefs, basic laws	3
compare and contrast	Hinduism, Buddhism, and Jainism	3
make a time line	of the history of the Indus Valley	any number
	of the history of Hinduism	any number
	of the history of Buddhism	any number
investigate	the what, when, where, why/how of: • the ancient cities of Mohenjo-daro and Harappa • Vedas, or Books of Knowledge	4
	the who, what, when, where of: • Siddhartha Gautama, founder of Buddhism	4
research	the rise and decline of the Mogul Empire in India and compare it to the rise and decline of the British Empire	any number

Huang He Valley

Skill	Activity Suggestion	Foldable Parts
K-W-L	write about what you know, want to know, and what you learn about the Huang-He Valley	3
locate and describe	the Huang River (Yellow River), the Chang Jiang (Yangtze), and the Xi-Jiang (West River)	3
trace	the route of the Huang River from its beginning on the Tibetan Plateau, through northern China, and into the Yellow Sea in the Pacific Ocean	4
make a concept map	of two dangers facing early Chinese civilizations • floods • raids from Huns or Mongols	2
investigate	levees and their use along the Huang River	2
compare and contrast	two ways of life in ancient China—farming along rivers and herding on the steppes	2
	the legendary first dynasty, Hsia with the historical first dynasty, Shang	2
research	the Shang dynasty, its development in the Huang River delta, and its rule from 1700 B.C. to 1100 B.C.	3
	bronze casting during the Shang dynasty	1
compare and contrast	the Shang dynasty and the Zhou dynasty	2
	Confucianism, Taoism, and Legalism	3
show cause and effect	of the Mandate of Heaven	2
research	development of iron weapons, the infantry, and the cavalry during the Period of Warring States	3
explain	how Shi Huanghi, Qin dynasty emperor, unified China through standardization and the building of the Great Wall of China, 3rd century	2
chart	the advances made during the 400 year Han dynasty in science, mathematics, the arts, and trade	any number
explain	effects of Confucianism on life during the Han dynasty	any number
research	fall of the Han dynasty and the division of China rule between the Wei, Shu, and Wu	3
search the web	the what, when, where, why or how of: • the Great Wall of China • oracle bones • origins of Taoism	4
	the who, what, when, where of: • mummy of Fu Hao, woman found in a royal tomb in Anyang • Confucius	4
make a chart	of inventions and technology of ancient China	2
make a timeline	of some of the dynasties of ancient China and note key events in China's history:	any number
	of the history of Ancient China	any number
	of the history of Chinese writing	any number
	of the history of silk	any number

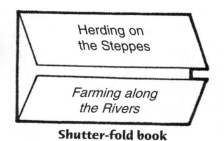

Shutter-fold book

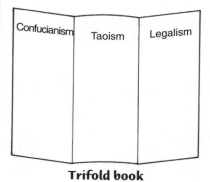

Trifold book

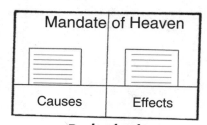

Pocket book

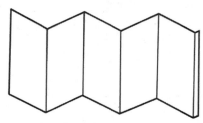

Timeline: History of the Great Wall of China

Bound book

The Spread of Civilization

Nomadic People	Settled People

1x2 Chart

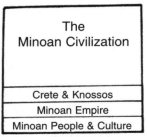

The
Minoan Civilization

Crete & Knossos

Minoan Empire

Minoan People & Culture

**Layer book
(2 sheets of paper)**

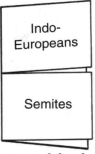

Indo-
Europeans

Semites

Two-tab book

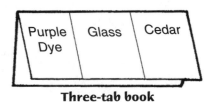

| Purple Dye | Glass | Cedar |

Three-tab book

| What | When | Where | Why |

Hanging Gardens
of
Babylon

Top-tab book

Skill	Activity Suggestion	Foldable Parts
investigate	ways in which nomadic people and settled people worked together and against one another	2
infer	how trade, migrations, and military interactions forced distant civilizations to interact	3
report on	the invention of the chariot (about 1700 BCE) and its use by warring people to conquer established civilizations	2
describe	the Minoan Civilization: • the island of Crete and its capital Knossos • the sea-based empire of the Minoans • the Minoan people and their culture	3
relate	theories concerning the end of the Minoan civilization and explain how their demise left the area vulnerable to the chariot warriors of Mycenae (Greek mainland) to dominate the region	2
know that	the Phoenicians are referred to by many names: • Sidonians, in the Old Testament of the Bible • Phoenicians by the Greek poet Homer • Semites, they were related to the Canaanites of ancient Palestine	3
compare and contrast	Indo-Europeans (crossed the Adriatic Sea about 1000 BCE, from the Balkan Peninsula and settled in central Italy) and Semites [ancient people who inhabited Aram, Assyria, Babylonia, Canaan (including the Hebrews), and Phoenicia]	2
	Hittites (Indo-European) and Egyptians as enemies and allies	2
show cause and effect	of the Indo European groups migrating into Europe, South Asia, and the Middle East	3
	of the defeat of the Hittites and the development of smaller kingdoms and city-states	2
research	three trade goods associated with the Phoenicians: • purple dye • glass • cedar	3
	Phoencian contributions to ocean exploration	any number
outline	the development of the 22 character Phoenician alphabet into our 26 character alphabet	1
research	Phoenician city of Carthage, founded 800s BCE • two natural harbors of Carthage • Carthage as the center of Phoenician shipping and trade • Phoenician armies use of Carthage to launch armies against Greece and Rome	any number
investigate	the who, what, when, where/why of the following • Hamilcar Barca • Hannibal • Sir Arthur Evans, British archaeologist • Minos the legendary king of the Minoans	4
	the seven wonders of the ancient world: • pyramids of Egypt • the 'hanging' gardens of Semiramis at Babylon • the statue of Zeus at Olympia • the temple of Artemis • the Mausoleum at Halicarnassus • the Colossus of Rhodes • the Pharos, or lighthouse at Alexandria, Egypt	7

Ancient Greece

Skill	Activity Suggestion	Foldable Parts
show cause and effect	of geography on Greek history	2
Venn Diagram	Egyptian society, Minoan society, both	3
investigate	the what, where, when, why/how of: • the legend of the Minotaur • the Lighthouse of Alexandria • Magna Graecia (colonies founded by Greek city states) • the first Olympic games, 778 BCE • the Persian Wars, 492, BCE • the Peloponnesian Wars	4
	the who, what, when, where of: • Philip of Macedon • Alexander the Great • Socrates • Sir Arthur Evans, archaeologist	4
describe	the palace at Knossos: past and present	2
compare and contrast	the Minoans and the Mycenaeans	2
show cause and effect	of collapse of the Mycenaean civilization	2
outline	the development of democracy in Athens	any number
explain	two key events during the Dark Age of Greece	2
compare and contrast	the city states of Athens and Sparta	2
define	monarchy, oligarchy, and democracy	3
explain	three reasons for the decline of nobility	3
	four ideas key to the Greek view of life	4
define	"tyrant" in terms of ancient Greece	1
research	four important statesmen, Solon, Pisistratus, Cleisthenes, Pericles, others	4
make a timeline	of the conflict between Greece and Persia during the Persian reigns of Darius I, II, and III	any number
show cause and effect	of decline of Athens	2
describe	Greece, before, during, and after Macedonia rule	3
Venn diagram	Plato's *The Republic*, Aristotle's *Politics,* both	3
research	five Greek philosophers: Socrates, Plato, Aristotle Epicurus, and Zeno	5
	Greek achievements in mathematics, science, philosophy, art, and architecture	5
compare and contrast	Greek historian--Homer, Herodotus and Thucydides	3
	Greek script, Egyptian hieroglyphics, and Babylonic cuneiform	3
	the Athenian League of city-states and the Peloponnesian League	2
determine	why Greek history is a series of wars between state and leagues of cities	1
	why the city-states of Greece became easy prey for Alexander the Great and, later, the Romans	2
describe	Greece during the Byzantine Empire (4th century AD) and later during the Ottoman Empire (13th century AD)	2

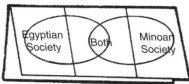

Three-tab Venn diagram

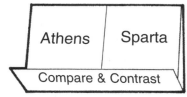

Two-tab matchbook

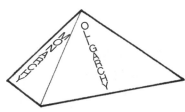

Pyramid fold

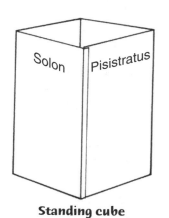

Standing cube

Trifold book

Pyramid fold

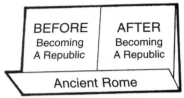

The Roman Empire

Skill	Activity Suggestion	Foldable Parts
K-W-L	write about what you know, want to know, and what you learn about Ancient Rome	3
locate	Ancient Rome on a historic map and modern Rome on a political map	2
note	the geography of Italy--mountains and plains--and research the Alps, the Apennines Mountains, and the Latium Plain	3
describe	the geography of Ancient Rome and how it contributed to the development of Roman culture	2
research	the Etruscans and explain how they created a unified Italy	2
tell	the legend of Romulus and Remus and the founding of Rome	1
compare and contrast	government in Ancient Rome before and after it became a republic	2
	views of the patricians and the plebeians	2
explain	why Rome is called the City of Seven Hills	1
	the three branches of the Republic of Rome— Senate, the citizen assembly, and the consuls	3
show cause and effect	of the Punic Wars and the defeat of Carthage	2
list	three examples of Roman contributions to the world	3
describe	the period in Roman history called Pax Romana	1
	how the line of succession to the throne of the Roman Empire was determined	1
outline	the rise and spread of Christianity during the Pax Roman	2
	how troubles within and outside the Roman Empire lead to the decline of the Roman Empire	2
	the rise and fall of the Roman Empire	2
make a concept map	Roman Empire—building an empire and governing an empire	2
	Rome--eastern and western empires	2
make a chart	of ways in which Ancient Rome influences the modern world through government, architecture, and language	3
make a timeline	of the history of the Roman Empire	any number
investigate	the what, when, where, why or how of: • Colosseum • Pantheon • gladiators	4
	the who, what, when, where of: • the Etruscan king Lars Porsenna • Marius and Sulla, 107-79 BC • Julius Caesar • Cleopatra • Augustus • Constantine	4
chart	key events in the lives of Crassus, Pompey, and Julius Caesar	any number
	events you consider to be "highs" and "lows" of the Roman Empire	2

Two-tab matchbook

Picture-frame book

Layer book (2 sheets of paper)

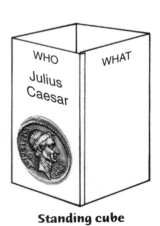

Standing cube

Judaism. Christianity, and Islam

Skill	Activity Suggestion	Foldable Parts
define	monotheism and describe the following faiths as monotheistic: Islam, Judaism, and Christianity	3
make a timeline	of any or all of the following: • the history of Judaism • the history of Christianity • the history of Islam	any number
make a table	and record the importance of Jerusalem to all three religions and past and present problems this mutual interest causes	3
compare	the holy books of the three religions: • the Torah, the holy book of Judaism • the Bible, the holy book of Christianity • the Quran, the holy book of Islam	3
search the web	for information on holy days for each religion: • Jewish holy days--Rosh Hashanah, Yom Kippur • Christian holy days--Easter, Christmas • Islamic holy days--Ramadan, Festival of Ashura	3
locate on a map	the birthplace of and the early route of each religion and understand factors that contributed to their spread	2
graph	the number of worldwide followers for each religion	3
investigate	the who, what, when, where of the following for Judaism: • Hebrew patriarchs: Abraham, Isaac, Jacob • Hebrew kings: Saul, David, and Solomon	4
	the who, what, when, where of the following for Christianity: • Jesus Christ • disciples: Peter, Paul, John, Mark, Matthew, others	4
	the who, what, when, where of the following for Islam: • Mohammed • the rightly guided caliphs (the successors of Muhammad)	4
investigate	the what, where, when, why/how of the following for Judaism: • Dead Sea Scrolls • the Ten Commandments and Mt. Sinai • the Diaspora	4
	the what, where, when, why/how of the following for Christianity: • the Crucification of Christ • the Crusades	4
	the what, where, when, why/how of the following for Islam: • the Hijrah, A.D. 622 • jihad • Makkah (Mecca)	4
research	the Hebrew people from Mesopotamia who first practiced Judaism	1
outline	the nomadic Hebrew tribes' quest for the "promised land" under the leaderships of Abraham and Moses	2
show cause and effect	of the division of the Hebrew kingdom into Israel and Judah	2
explain	the Diaspora, or "scattering of the Jews outside the Holy Land" and give examples	2

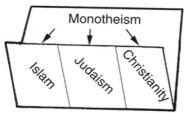

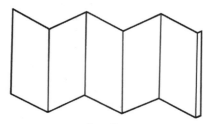

Three-tab concept map

Timeline:
History of Judaism

Religion	Importance of Jerusalem	Past Conflicts	Present Conflicts
Judaism			
Islam			
Christianity			

4x4 Folded chart

King Saul	King David	King Solomon

1x3 Chart

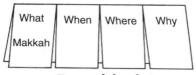

Four-tab book

Moslem Empire

K-W-L	write about what you know, want to know, and what you learn about the Arab World	3
locate	past and present Moslem Empire on a map and globe	2
show cause and effect	of desert land and desert oases	2
trace	trade routes linking Arabia with Egypt and the Fertile Crescent on a map	any number
research	The Five Pillars of Islam	5
	the sacred month of Ramadan	1
describe	what you think might happen before, during, and after a pilgrimage	3
explain	how the spread of the Islamic Empire enriched and was enriched by other civilizations	2
	caliph and caliphate	3
Venn diagram	Roman Empire, Islamic Empire, both	3
compare and contrast	the beliefs of Muslims and any other religion: Buddhists, Hindus, Christians, Jews, others…	2
make a chart	showing the achievements of the Caliphate in: medicine, math and science, architecture, and literature	5
make a timeline	on the history of Jerusalem	any number
	the history of the Crusades	any number
investigate	the what, when, where, why or how of: • Mecca • Kaaba • Quran • the Dome of the Rock (mosque in Jerusalem) • Sufism and Sufi poetry	4
	the who, what, when, where of: • the prophet Muhammed • Haroun al-Rashid, an Abbasid caliph	4
make a timeline	the key events in the rise of Islam, 612 AD to 1500AD: • 612 AD, the Prophet Muhammad began to preach in Mecca • 622, Muhammad was forced to flee to Medina • 630, Muhammad and an alliance of tribes captured Mecca which became the capital of the empire • 632, Muhammad died • 632, most of Arabia was Muslim by this date • 632, Muhammad succeeded by the caliph Abu Bakr • 634, Abu Bakr died and was succeeded by Omar • 632-644, conquest of the Middle East by the caliphs • 644, Omar assassinated and succeeded by Othman who wrote the first version of the Qur'an. • 661, civil war, power seized by the Umayyads and the capital of the empire moved to Damascus • 661-750, Damascus center of Islam • 750, Ummayads overthrown by Abbasids who built Baghdad, a walled city with four gates • 1096, start of the Crusades • 1187, Saladin captured the city of Jerusalem • 1303, last Crusaders left Islamic Empire • 1453, Ottoman Turks conquered Islamic Empire	any number

Shutter-fold book
Shiites | Sunnis

Layer book (3 sheets of paper)
Five Pillars of Islam
Iman
Salah
Zakah
Sawm
Hajj

Top-tab book
Medicine | Math & Science | Architecture | Literature
Achievements of the Caliphate

Picture-frame book
Dome Rock

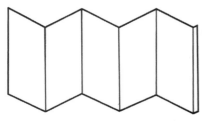

Timeline: History of Islam

Feudalism and the Middle Ages

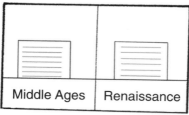

Pocket book

Skill	Activity Suggestion	Foldable Parts
K-W-L	write about what you know, want to know, and what you learn about Feudalism and the Middle Ages	3
locate	Europe on a historic map and compare and contrast it to the Europe of today	2
compare and contrast	the Middle Ages and the Renaissance	2
	the life of each of the following: king, baron, knight, villeins (peasant who owns some land), cottars peasants who own a cottage), and bordars, (peasants who owned next to nothing)	6
find similarities and differences	between serfs and slaves	2
	between feudalism in England and feudalism in France and Russia	2
use	and define the terms Middle Ages, Medieval times, and Dark Ages	3
show cause and effect	of the growth of towns and trade	2
determine	how Christianity affected life during this time	any number
	how knights were "recruited" to go on Crusades	1
outline	the history of the Crusades	any number
explain	the relations between the Christians and the Jews in Europe at this time	2
	how the Renaissance was a mixture of old and new knowledge	2
	how *homage* (usually a religious ceremony in which a baron swears to obey and defend his king) effected the lives of barons for better and for worse	2
write	five journal entries from an imaginary pilgrimage	5
	about the life of a peasant in Feudal England (they had to pay taxes to their lord, work for the lord, ask for the lord's permission to marry, ask before leaving the lord's property)	any number
research	the cause and effect of the Black Death	2
	why and how barons and knights had to perform military service for the king	2
describe	how land determined one's wealth and power	2
	how over time fewer people began to own the majority of the land	2
make a concept map	manors—serfs, knights, vassals, lord and lady	4
	Christian Church divided into the Eastern Orthodox Church and the Roman Catholic Church	2
	the Reformation resulted in Roman Catholicism and Protestantism	2
investigate	the "what, when, where, why or how" of: • the Black Death, 1348 • the Magna Carter, 1215 • Norman Invasion • the War of Roses, 1455 to 1485	4
investigate	the "who, what, when, where" of the following: • Charlemagne • William the Conqueror • King John I • Henry VI, and the end of Feudalism in England	4

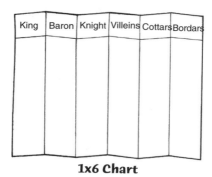

1x6 Chart

Three-tab concept map

Causes of the Black Death / Effects of the Black Death

Two-tab book

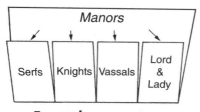

Four-tab concept map

Ancient Africa

Five-tab book

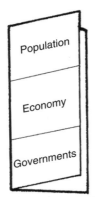

Three-tab book

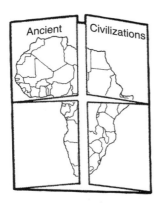

Four-door book

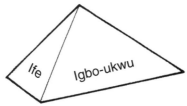

Pyramid fold

Standing cube

Skill	Activity Suggestion	Foldable Parts
K-W-L	write about what you know, want to know, and what you learn about ancient African civilizations	3
locate	ancient African civilizations on a historic map and using a political map, note what countries are currently located in these regions	2
investigate	Africa's mountains, rivers, deserts, grasslands, forests	5
	ancient Africa's population, economy, governments	3
research	ancient societies of Africa clustered around each of the following important bodies of water: the Niger river, the Nile river, the Congo River, the Red Sea, and the Indian Ocean	5
compare and contrast	Saharan Africa and Subsaharan Africa— past and present	4
explain	how and why livestock wealth and interregional trade influenced the growth of societies in Saharan and Subsaharan Africa	2
	why Africa is often said to be "The Cradle of Civilization" and give specific examples	2
Venn diagram	Kush, Ancient Egypt, both	3
describe	the empires and the known history of Northwest Africa, West Africa, East Africa, and South Africa	4
appreciate	griots, past and present, for their contributions to the preservation of Africa's oral history	2
make a table to	record information on Mombasa, Zanzibar, and Mogadishu—past and present	6
	Pre-Aksumite and Aksumite civilization, Ethiopia	2
show cause and effect	of trade in ivory, gold, and slaves	3
search the web	for information on early civilizations in Great Zimbabwe	any number
make a chart	Africa's Eastern Coast—location, resources, needs and wants, trade	4
make a table	showing the accomplishments of the independent kingdoms of Kush, Aksum, and Zagwe in northeastern Africa	3
make a concept map	Western Empires Rich in Gold—Ghana, Mali, Songhai	3
describe	Igbo-ukwu, Ife, and Benin, in West Africa	3
make a timeline	of the history of ancient Africa	any number
investigate	the what, when, where, why or how of: • Rock Churches of Lalibela • Timbuktu • the Great Mosque of Kilwa, 11th century • Napata, in present-day Sudan, center of the Kushite state from about 860 to 270 b.c.e. • stelae of Aksum • rock-city of Great Zimbabwe	4
	the who, what, when, where of: • King Mansa Musa	4

Ancient Americas

Skill	Activity Suggestion	Foldable Parts
K-W-L	write about what you know, want to know, and what you learn about ancient American civilizations	3
locate on a map	the prehistoric land bridge, Beringia, and the current Bering Strait	2
	the states in the Four Corners region of the U.S.	4
Venn diagram	Beringia, Bering Strait, both	3
make a table	of the past and present geography and climate of North America, Middle America, and South America	3
research and report on	three Anasazi, or ancestral Pueblo (the ancient farmers of the Southwest) ruins	3
	past and present theories about the Mississippian, or the mound-building farming societies that lived in Eastern America	2
explain	two reasons why people might migrate from one area to another: climate, hunting, escape enemies, other	2
chart and describe	three or more achievements of the Olmec, Maya, Aztec, and Inca	4+
investigate	the purpose and importance of astronomy to the Maya	2
	the purpose and use of the kiva by the Anasazi	2
make a concept map	Middle American Civilizations: Olmec, Maya, Aztec	3
speculate	as to the reasons for the rise and decline of the Anasazi and Mississippian societies	2
make a timeline	of the history of ancient American Civilizations: • Olmecs, 1200 BCE, Gulf of Mexico • Mayas, 1000 BCE, Southern Mexico • Chavin, 700-200 BCE, Andes • Zapotecs, 200 AD, Oaxaca Valley of Mexico • Toltecs, 930 AD • Aztecs, 1325 AD • Incas, 1513 AD	any number
investigate	the "what, when, where, why or how" of • the ice age • Chichén itzá • Tenochtitlan • chinampas, floating gardens of the Aztec • ancient Olmec city of La Venta (Mexico) • Canyon de Chelly and Chaco Canyon • Mesa Verde • Cahokia, the largest city in pre-Columbian North America	4
report on	pre-Columbian Native Americans living in the NE, SE, NW, and SW, regions of the current US, including information on the geography of the region and their use of resources to meet their basic needs	4
describe	the importance of "the three sisters": maize, beans, and squash to Native Americans	3

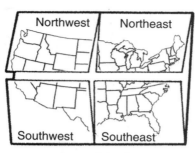

Four-door book

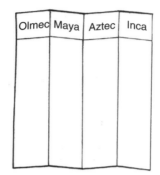

4x1 Folded chart

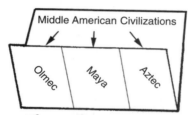

Three-tab concept map

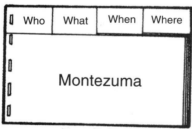

Top-tab book

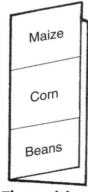

Three-tab book

The Renaissance and Reformation

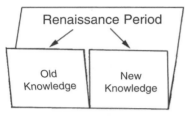

Three-tab book

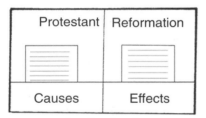

Two-tab concept map

Skill	Activity Suggestion	Foldable Parts
K-W-L	write about what you know, want to know, and what you learn about the Renaissance	3
explain	two ways in which the decline of feudalism helped begin the Renaissance about A.D. 1350	2
make a chart	outlining the accomplishments of the Middle Ages and the Renaissance	2
	of information on the Middle Ages, the Renaissance, and the Reformation	3
track	how the Renaissance spread from northern Italy into Europe and explain the movement	2
explain	how the Renaissance was a mixture of old and new knowledge	2
investigate	the who, what, when, where of Renaissance Artists: • Filippo Brunelleschi • Donato di Niccolò di Betto Bardi • Leonardo da Vinci • Michelangelo Buonarotti • Jacopo Bellin	4
	the who, what, when, where of Renaissance writers: • Geoffrey Chaucer • Miguel de Cervantes • William Shakespeare	4
	the who, what, when, where of the Protestant Reformation: • Martin Luther • John Calvin	4
analyze	the causes and effects of the Protestant Reformation	2
show cause and effect	of the beginning of the Renaissance and increased interest in exploration	2
make a concept map	Reformation--altered Roman Catholicism and created Protestantism	2
	illustrating how and why the Christian Church divided into Eastern Orthodox Church and the Roman Catholic Church	2
determine	two ways in which science changed during this time	2
report on	the life and death of Nicolaus Copernicus	2
make a timeline	of key events in the Reformation: • 1482-1492, Pope Innocent VIII • 1492-1503, Pope Alexander VI • 1482-1503, papacy criticized and found to be corrupt • 1500's, protests began against the Catholic Church called the "Reformation" • 1517, Johann Tetzel was selling indulgences from the Pope and Martin Luther, Wittenberg University professor, said indulgences could not be bought • 1521, Diet of Worms, Luther defended his views, but was still banned from Catholic church (this led to the founding of the Lutheran Church) • 1542, Universal Inquisition started by Pope Paul III • 1568, Dutch Revolt against Rome and the Inquisition was the first of many wars between Catholics in southern Europe and Protestants in northern Europe	any number

Protestant | Reformation

Causes | Effects

Pocket book

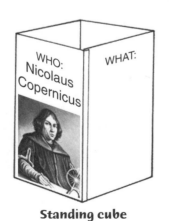

WHO: Nicolaus Copernicus

WHAT:

Standing cube

The Age of Discovery

Skill	Activity Suggestion	Foldable Parts
K-W-L	write about what you know, want to know, and what you learn about exploration and discovery beginning in the late 1400's	3
cause and effect	of advances in sailing technologies and the beginning of an age of exploration: • astrolabe, • magnetic • compass, • new materials used for sails, others	2
	of the empires of America being conquered by Spain	2
list	pros and cons of exploration and expansion	4
define	caravel, strait, conquistador, missionary, convert	5
locate	on a map or globe: • Strait of Magellan • Portugal • Italy • Spain	any number
investigate	the who, what, when, where of the following: • Marco Polo • Prince Henry of Portugal • Bartolomeu Dias • Christopher Columbus • Vasco da Gama • Ferdinand Magellan • Pedro Alvarez Cabral • Hernando Cortes • Moctezuma • Francisco Pizarro • Atahualpa, emperor of Inca empire • James Cook, others	4
research	the "what, where, when, why/how" of: • the Line of Demarcation, 1494	4
make a chart	of explorers, their lives, achievements, and adventures	4
make a table	of explorers, dates, routes, discoveries	any number
make a timeline	of the history of exploration by sea	any number
	of European exploration of the Americas	any number
	of the development of slavery in the Americas	any number
explain	why Europeans wanted to find a cheaper route to Asia	1
list	five difficulties faced by early explorers	5
	three difficulties faced by a nation ruling distant lands	3
compare and contrast	past and present attitudes towards nations taking the land of another nation	2
	American land claimed by Spain and land claimed by Portugal in the year 1600	2
describe	how trade goods, people, diseases, and knowledge moved worldwide through the Columbian Exchange	4
research	the Line of Demarcation, drawn in 1494	1
	and explain the triangular trade route between West Indies, Africa, and Europe: trade of sugar, European goods, and slaves	3
describe	how life for the conquered people in the Americas was shaped by missionaries, mining, and farm work	3
	prehistoric peoples as explorers	1
discover	two important reasons for English colonization of Australia	2
Venn diagram	of Spanish Exploration, Portuguese Exploration, both	3

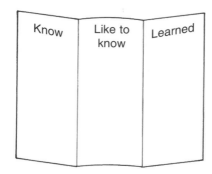

Trifold book

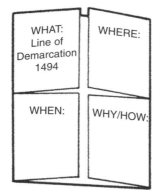

Four-door book

The Age of Discovery

Caravel
Strait
Conquistador
Missionary
Convert

Layer book
(3 sheets of paper)

Who	What	When	Where
Marco Polo			
Vasco de Gama			
Hernando Cortes			

4x4 Folded chart

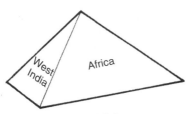

Pyramid fold

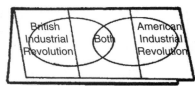

Three-tab Venn diagram

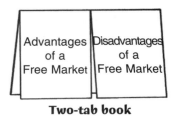

Two-tab book

Top-tab book

Bound book

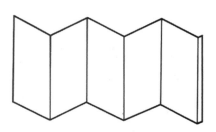

Timeline:
of the Industrial Revolution

The Industrial Revolution

Skill	Activity Suggestion	Foldable Parts
K-LK-L	ask yourself what you know, what you would like to know, and review what you learn about the Industrial Revolution	3
show	cause and effect of the Industrial Revolution	2
make a Venn diagram	of the British Industrial Revolution, the American Industrial Revolution, both	3
list	ways in which the Industrial Revolution changed how people live and work	2
speculate	as to why the Industrial Revolution began in America about 1790, shortly after the American Revolution	any number
discuss	at least three reasons why the Industrial Revolution began in New England and flourished there: • large work force • good ports • natural resources available • water power harnessed to run machinery • capitalism and free-enterprise encouraged industry	3+
chart	positive and negative effects of the Industrial Revolution	2
	advantages and disadvantages of a free market	2
investigate	how the Industrial Revolution changed transportation on land and on water	2
	four inventions that strengthened the Industrial Revolution	4
explain	how faster production lowers costs of products and the importance of interchangeable parts	2
show	the cause and effect of lower transportation costs and increased trade	2
investigate	the who, what, when, and where of one of the following: • Samuel Slater • Eli Whitney • Francis Cabot Lowell • Cyrus McCormick • John Deere • Robert Fulton	4
research	Massachusetts as the leading manufacturing state in the early 1800's, and determine the leading manufacturing state today	2
write	7 days of journal entries describing daily life as a worker in a factory	7
make a timeline	of the Industrial Revolution's beginning in Great Britain and growth in America: • 1730s, shift from cottage production to machine production due to new inventions • 1759, an artificial waterways were built to transport • 1785 steam engine powered a cotton mill • 1793 Eli Whitney invented the cotton gin • 1789 Samuel Slater came to America from England and produced thread using the designs from Richard Arkwright's thread machines • 1790 patent law passed by Congress • 1814 Francis Cabot Lowell developed a way to produce everything in one location, giving birth to the factory, and more	any number

Imperialism

Skill	Activity Suggestion	Foldable Parts
define and differentiate between	imperialism and colonialism • *colonialism* "usually implies formal political control, involving territorial annexation and loss of sovereignty" • *imperialism* is a "control or influence that is exercised either formally or informally, directly or indirectly, politically or economically"	2
chart and list	the pros and cons of each of the main reasons for imperialism: political reasons, economic reasons, ideological reasons	3
compare	the empire of Alexander the Great and the Roman Empire as examples of imperialism in the ancient world	2
	French and British imperialism in the 1800's	2
research and report on	10 key events occurring during the early modern period of European imperialism (1400-1750) (Note: this period was predominantly overseas colonial expansion with competing countries trying to control territories in parts of Asia and the New World.)	10
determine	how imperialist countries controlled the trade of their colonies, and reaped the benefits of that trade	2
	why by the end of the 19th century, European powers had expanded into each of the following: Africa, Asia, and the Pacific, or Oceania	3
explain	"economic imperialism" or powerful countries using their economic power over international financial organizations to control other countries	1
debate	whether *neocolonialism* does or does not exist today (former Imperialistic powers continuing to affect the politics and the economics of former colonies)	2
make a table	of African colonies, date of colonization, date of independence, important events and/or people	any number
make a concept map	India before, during, and after colonization	3
describe	how Southeast Asia's independence resulted in Vietnam, Laos, and Cambodia	3
make a time line	of the history of colonization of Africa of the Israeli-Palestinian conflict of the Jewish struggle for a homeland	any number
sequence	the events leading to India's independence	any number
list	three changes that the British East India Company brought to the Indian subcontinent	3
investigate	the lives of Mohandas Gandhi, Jawaharlal Nehru, and Indira Gandhi	3
research	how the nations in Southeast Asia gained independence from France, Britain, and Netherlands	3
explain	two effects of European colonialism on Africa	2
	why more than 100 nations have gained independence since 1943	
	reactive imperialism using the British conquest of India and the Russian colonization of Central Asia in the 19th century as examples	2

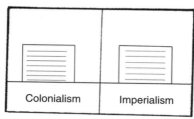

Pocket book

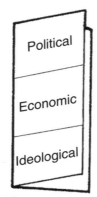

Three-tab book

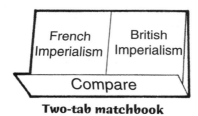

Two-tab matchbook

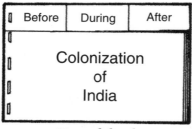

Top-tab book

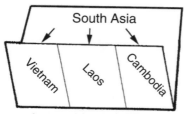

Three-tab concept map

World War I

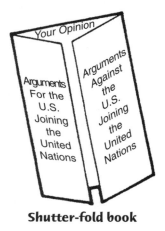

Allied	Central

1x2 Chart

World Before	Events and During	WWI After

Trifold book

Your Opinion

Arguments For the U.S. Joining the United Nations

Arguments Against the U.S. Joining the United Nations

Shutter-fold book

Zeppelin

Picture-frame book

Skill	Activity Suggestion	Foldable Parts
K-LK-L	ask yourself what you know, what you would like to know, and review what you learn about World War I	3
compare	the Allied Powers and the Central Powers	2
locate	the following on a map or globe: Britain, France, Italy, Belgium and Russia (Allies)	5
	Germany, Austria-Hungary, Turkey (Central Powers)	3
explain	two key events that led the United States into WWI	2
outline	three things Woodrow Wilson said the United States should fight for	3
describe	two ways in which World War I changed the United States	2
	world events before, during, and after WWI	3
research	the design and use of German U-boats, war planes, and tanks	3
debate	the use of poison gas as a weapon	1
argue	for and against the United States joining the League of Nations after World War I	2
list	examples of difficulties faced on the war front and the home front of two different countries	2
investigate	the who, what, when, where of one of the following: • Archduke Franz Ferdinand • Woodrow Wilson • Eddie Rickenbacker, American pilot • Baron von Richthofen, "Red Baron," German pilot	4
	the what, where, when, why/how, of one of the following: • Lusitania • Zimmermann telegram • the Treaty of Versailles (1919) • the League of Nations • Veteran's Day	4
research	and report on one of the military firsts of WWI: • use of poison gas • armored tanks • airplanes • zeppelins, or blimps • others	
Venn diagram	Civil War submarines, German U-boats, both	3
make a time line	of some of the key events of World War I • 1914, June 28 Franz Ferdinand was assassinated • 1914, June World War I began • 1914, August 23 Japan declared war on Germany • 1914, September Battle of the Marne • 1914, April poison gas first used by the Germans • 1915, May Lusitania torpedoed by Germany • 1916, Battle of Verdun Battle of Somme • 1916, January armored tanks first used in war • 1917, the dancer 'Mata Hari' was shot by the French as a German spy • 1917, United States entered the war • 1918, Battle of the Argonne Forest • 1918, November 11 World War I ended • 1919, Treaty of Versailles signed • 1920, U.S. Senate rejected League of Nations	any number

World War II

Skill	Activity Suggestion	Foldable Parts
K-LK-L	ask yourself what you know, what you would like to know, and review what you learn about World War II	3
sequence	four events contributing to the start of the war in Europe	4
	three events that occurred on December 7, 1941	3
compare and contrast	World War II before and after United States involvement	2
	democracy and communism	2
list	pros and cons of United States involvement	2
locate	the following on a map or globe: • Pearl Harbor, Island of Oahu, Hawaii • Hiroshima, Japan • Nagasaki, Japan	4
differentiate	between the Axis countries and the Allied countries	2
make a concept map	on dictators--Hitler, Stalin, and Mussolini	3
	on World War II Fronts--Pacific/Asian and European	2
	of World War II Countries--Axis, Allied, Neutral	3
describe	the world economy before, during, and after World War II	3
	the goals of the United Nations--past and present	2
outline	arguments for and against the use of relocation camps	2
research	four battles of World War II	4
list	three lasting effects of World War II on the world	3
research	the who, what, when, where of one of the following: • Franklin D. Roosevelt • Winston Churchill • Adolf Hitler • Dwight D. Eisenhower • Josef Stalin • Harry S. Truman • Benito Mussolini	4
	the what, where, when, why/how of one of the following: • Pearl Harbor • atomic bomb • Holocaust • concentration camps	4
make a timeline	of some key events of World War II: • 1939, September 1 World War II began, Hitler (Germany) invades Poland • 1940, August Germany bombed Britain • 1941, June Hitler attacked the Soviet Union • 1941, December 7 Japan bombed Pearl Harbor • 1941, December U.S. declared war on Japan • 1941, December Germany and Italy, allies of Japan, declared war on U.S. • 1942, January United States joined Allies • 1942, April Allies surrendered Bataan • 1944, June 6 Battle of Normandy, D-Day Invasion • 1944, December Battle of the Bulge • 1945, March Battle of Iwo Jima • 1945, June Battle of Okinawa • 1945, August Atomic bomb dropped on Hiroshima • 1945, May Germany surrendered • 1945, August 15 V-J Day, "Victory over Japan" • 1945, September 3 Japan's formal surrender • World War II ends • 1945, October United Nations formed	any number

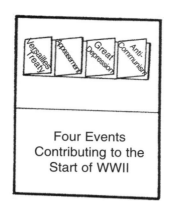

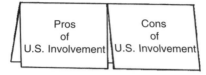

Four Events Contributing to the Start of WWII

Billboard project

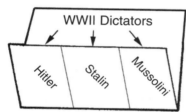

Pros of U.S. Involvement | Cons of U.S. Involvement

Two-tab book

WWII Dictators

Hitler | Stalin | Mussolini

Three-tab concept map

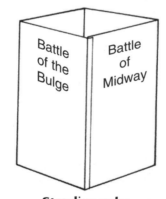

Battle of the Bulge | Battle of Midway

Standing cube

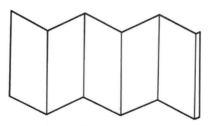

Timeline:
Key Events of WWII

Mainland Europe

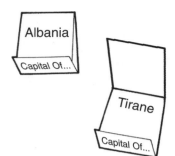

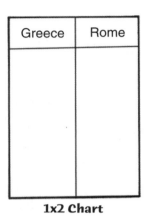

1x2 Chart

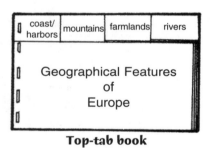

Top-tab book

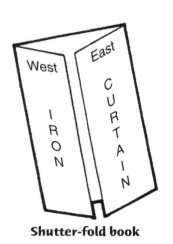

Shutter-fold book

Skill	Activity Suggestion	Foldable Parts
locate	the following countries and their capital cities on a world map: • Albania • Andorra • Austria • Belarus • Belgium • Bosnia and Herzegovina • Bulgaria • Croatia • Cyprus • Czech Republic • Denmark • Estonia • Finland • France • Germany • Greece • Hungary • Iceland • Italy • Latvi • Liechtenstein • Lithuania • Luxembourg • Macedonia • Malta • Moldova • Monaco • Netherlands • Norway • Poland • Portugal • Romania • San Marino • Slovakia • Slovenia • Spain • Sweden • Switzerland • Ukraine • Vatican City • Yugoslavia • Wales	any number
chart	information on 10 of the countries in this area and determine what they have in common	10
determine	which countries once made up Classical Europe, or the civilizations of Greece and Rome	1
investigate	three or more geographic features of Europe: long coastlines, good harbors, mountains, farm land, navigable rivers, temperate climate	3+
	the who, what, when, where for the following: • the Habsburgs, Austrian royal family • Guiseppe Mazzini, Young Italy movement • Giuseppe Garibaldi, republican guerrilla leader • Otto von Bismarck, chancellor of Germany, 1862	4
	the what, when, where, why/how for the following: • Dutch East India Company (1602-1798) • the Zollverein, 1819 economic union • 1820s rise of nationalism • Delta Plan Project, 1986, Netherlands	4
locate	the following geographic locations and understand their importance to the area: Europe, Ural Mountains, Asia	3
	Mediterranean, Black, Baltic, Celtic, and North Seas	5
	Alps and Pyrenees Mountains	2
	Rhine and Danube rivers	2
	Italian, Iberian, Balkan Peninsulas	3
find cause and effect	of the following: • the political power associated with the atomic bomb • the Iron Curtain, 1945-1946	2
graph and compare	relations between the east and west sides of the North Atlantic before and after NATO	2

Mainland Europe

Make a time line of some of the key historic events taking place in this region since 1700:

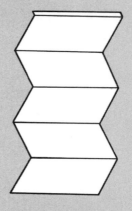

- 1789, French Revolution
- 1799, Napoleon Bonaparte, dictator of France
- 1800s Industrial Revolution spreads
- 1804, Napoleon appointed himself emperor of France
- 1815, Napoleon defeated, Battle of Waterloo
- 1848, Karl Marx published *Communist Manifesto*
- 1870-1871, Franco-Prussian War
- 1873, the DreiKaiserBund, the Three Emperors' League was signed by emperors of Austria, Germany, and Russia
- 1914, Austrian Archduke Ferdinand and his wife were shot by Serbian terrorist and World War I began
- 1918, WWI ended
- 1922, Benito Mussolini, Italian fascist dictator
- 1930s, worldwide depression
- 1933, Hitler became chancellor of Germany
- 1934, October 9: King Alexander I of Yugoslavia and French foreign minister Jean Louis Barthou were assassinated by a Macedonian terrorist in Marseilles
- 1934, Germany, Hitler assumed title "Der Fuhrer"
- 1936, Spanish Civil War, General Francisco Franco
- 1939, Axis powers at war with Allies in Europe
- 1941, U.S.A. and Soviet Union joined Allies
- 1942-1945, Holocaust took place during WWII
- 1944, July 20: Hitler survived assassination attempt
- 1945, World War II ends
- 1945, November 29: Yugoslavia became a republic
- 1947-1948, Cold War began in Europe U.S. began Marshall Plan to rebuild Europe GATT (General Agreement on Tariffs and Trades)
- 1949, NATO formed
- 1961, Berlin wall built between East and West Berlin
- 1975, General Franco died and Juan Carlos I became King of Spain
- 1989-1990, German reunification as Berlin Wall falls
- 1990s, Yugoslavia divided into five countries
- 1991, USSR divided into 15 independent republics, some in Europe
- 1991-1992, Wars in Yugoslavia; Slovenia and Croatia declared independence
- 1992, Serbs began policy of ethnic cleansing in Bosnia-Herzegovina
- 1993, European Union formed
- 1998, launch of the Euro
- 1999, crisis in Kosovo
- 2002, European Union began using a common currency, the Euro
- 2003, March 12 Serbian Prime Minister assassinated
- 2005, April 2 Pope John Paul II dies

Time Line

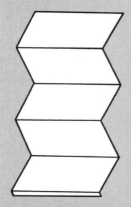

United Kingdom

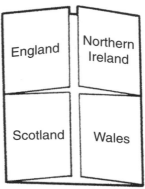

Four-door book

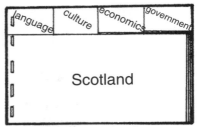

Top-tab book

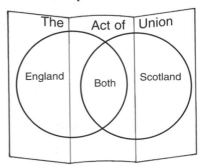

Trifold book

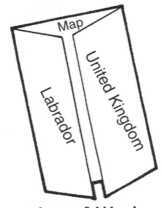

Shutter-fold book

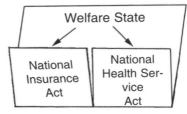

Two-tab concept map

Skill	Activity Suggestion	Foldable Parts
locate	the following countries and their capital cities on a world map: • England • Northern Ireland • Scotland • Wales	4
graph	information on each country in this area and determine what they have in common: • language • government • economics • culture	4
investigate	the who, what, when, where for the following: • Adam Smith, Scottish economist • David Hume, Scottish philosopher • Tobias Smollett, James Boswell, Robert Burns, and Sir Walter Scott, famous Scottish authors • Queen Victoria and Prince Albert • King Edward VIII, Duke of Windsor • Winston Churchill, Conservative Party • Margaret Thatcher, Conservative Party • Tony Blair, Labor Party • Queen Elizabeth II	4
	the what, when, where, why/how for the following: • the East India Company--original charter granted by Queen Elizabeth I in 1600, under the title of "The Governor and Company of Merchants of London Trading into the East Indies." • Scottish Enlightenment, 18th century • Guy Fawkes day	4
compare and contrast	Labrador and United Kingdom geographically	2
make a Venn diagram	to compare the land and culture of the highland zone, the lowland zone, and both	3
locate	the following geographic locations and understand their importance to the area: • Thames and the Severn rivers • Lough Neagh (Northern Ireland) and Loch Lomond, (Scotland)	2 2
explain why	the Labor Party wanted to create a welfare state after the war: • National Insurance Act • National Health Service Act	2
show cause and effect	WWII led to the dismantling of the British Empire	2
outline	the rise and fall of the British Empire	2
graph	by the late 1890's, about 25% of the world's land and people were controlled in (varying degrees) by the British Empire	2
graph	the land area of the UK: England, 54%; Scotland, 32%; Wales, 8%, and Northern Ireland, 6%	4
make a table	of information on 5 of the following: Anguilla, Bermuda, British Antarctic Territory, British Indian Ocean Territory, British Virgin Islands, Cayman Islands, Falkland Islands (Islas Malvinas), Gibraltar, Montserrat, Pitcairn Island, Saint Helena, South Georgia Islands, South Sandwich Islands, Turks and Caicos Islands	5

United Kingdom

Make a time line of some of the key historic events taking place in this region since 1700:

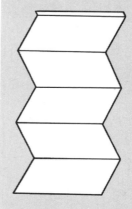

- 1707, The Act of Union created a single national administration for England and Scotland (forming Great Britain), removed trade barriers between the countries, standardized taxation throughout the island, and created a single Parliament, yet the countries continued to have separate traditions of law and separate official churches
- 1708, 1715, and 1745, Jacobite rebellions in Scotland, after the 1745 Rebellion the clan system in the Highlands was abolished
- 1775-1783, British monopoly on tobacco trade ended with American Revolution
- 1801, Act of Union, Great Britain and Ireland formed United Kingdom of Great Britain and Ireland
- 1805, October 21 Lord Admiral Nelson, mortally wounded at the Battle of Trafalgar
- 1807, slave trade abolished in British Empire
- 1810, London reached 1,000,000 in population, first city to do so in modern Europe
- 1812, War of 1812, Britain and United States
- 1821, famine in Ireland
- 1829, regular police force began patrolling London
- 1831-1835, Charles Darwin traveled to South America
- 1833, abolition of slavery in British Empire
- 1845-1850, Irish Famine
- 1847, 10-hour work day introduced
- 1860, August 30 first British tramway (by American, George F. Train)
- 1902-1904, period of 'Splendid Isolation' in British foreign policy ended
- 1902, Britain signed treaty with Japan
- 1904, Britain signed Entente Cordiale with France
- 1907, Britain signed entente with Russia
- 1912, Irish Revolution against British rule began
- 1916, September 3 Zeppelin shot down over England
- 1920, Government of Ireland Act
- 1921, Anglo-Irish Treaty
- 1925, Welsh nationalist party, Plaid Cymru, founded
- 1928, women were allowed to vote
- 1940, Battle of Britain
- 1940, rationing started in Britain
- 1949, the Republic of Ireland became an independent state, separate from British Commonwealth
- 1952, November 25 Agatha Christie's play, *The Mousetrap*, started the world's longest continuous run of any theatrical production
- 1953, fourteen years of sugar rationing ended
- 1954, food rationing ended nine years after WWII
- 1972, "Bloody Sunday" and then "Bloody Friday"
- 1973, Britain joined the EEC (European Union)
- 1978, world's first "test-tube" baby born in England and she gave birth to her first child in 2007.
- 1982, Falklands War
- 1993, Downing Street Declaration
- 1997, the Labour Party controlled the British government for the first time in 18 years
- 1997, three-fourths of the people of Scotland voted to create their own parliament
- 1997 Welsh voters supported the creation of a Welsh assembly--50.3% for and 49.7%against
- 1998, historic Northern Ireland peace agreement
- 1999, Scottish Parliament convened for the first time since 1707
- 1999, elections were held, the Welsh assembly convened the same year in Cardiff
- 2003, March Iraq War with American and British troops invaded Iraq
- 2005, May Tony Blair wins third successive term as Labour Prime Minister

Time Line

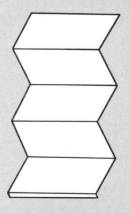

Russia and Eurasia Republics

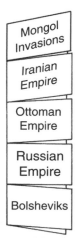

Five-tab book

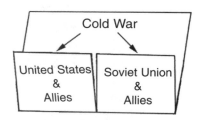

Skill	Activity Suggestion	Foldable Parts
locate	the following countries and their capital cities on a world map: • Armenia, Yerevan • Azerbaijan, Baku • Georgia, T'bilisi • Kazakhstan, Astana • Kyrgyzstan, Bishkek • Russia, Moscow • Tajikistan, Dushanbe • Turkmenistan, Ashgabat • Uzbekistan, Tashkent	any number
make a table	of information about each country in this area and determine what they have in common	9
explain	what influence each of the following had on the area: • Mongol Invasions • the Iranian Empire • the Ottoman Empire • the Russian Empire • the Bolsheviks (later known as the Communists)	5
outline	the history of the Cossacks (frontier settlers) from Russia who first settled along the Ural River in the 16th century	any number
	the history of the Kazakhs who are descendants of Mongol and Turkic people	any number
investigate	the who, what, when, where for the following: • Czar Nicholas II • Vladimir Lenin • Joseph Stalin • Nikita Khrushchev • Leonid Brezhnev, 1964-1982 • Yuri Andropov, 1982-1984 • Konstantin Chernenko, 1984-1985 • Mikhail Gorbachev, 1985-	4
	the what, when, where, why/how for the following: • Central Asian Republics • Iron Curtain countries • the Cold War	4
locate	the following geographic locations and understand their importance to the area: • Ural Mountains, Caucasus Mountains • Arctic Ocean • Black Sea, Caspian Sea • Lake Baikal • Volga River	5
give	two reasons the United States is opposed to Russia and Cuba having strong political alliances	2
research and report on	life for Armenians under the Ottoman Empire and the Russian Empire during the 19th and early 20th centuries	2
make a table	to compare political and economic conditions in three countries in the years before and after 1991	3
research	a former premier (such as Nikita S. Khrushchev) of Russia and explain why this position was eliminated in 1990	2

Layer book
(3 sheets of paper)

Two-tab concept map

3x4 Folded chart

Russia and Eurasia Republics

Make a time line of some of the key historic events taking place in this region since 1800:

- 1812, Napoleon and French army invaded Russia and were defeated by Russian soldiers
- 1853-1855, Crimean War
- 1853, Kazakhstan became conquest of Russia
- 1893, the Russian composer Tchaikovsky died
- 1904, Russo-Japanese War
- 1911, Russian premier, Peter Stolypin, shot by an assassin in Kiev theatre in front of tsar and tsarina
- 1914, War with Germany
- 1915, Tsar Nicholas II, as commander-in-chief, is blamed by his people for Russian failures
- 1916, Gregory Rasputin, monk advisor to Tsarina Alexandra, was murdered
- 1917, the February Revolution
- 1917, March 2 Tsar Nicholas abdicated
- 1917, November 7 "the October Revolution" when the Marxists Bolsheviks took power in Russia
- 1918, Vladimir Lenin, became dictator
- 1922, Azerbaijan, Georgia, and Armenia became part of the Union of Soviet Socialist Republics
- 1924-1953, Joseph Stalin--new communist leader
- 1928, Stalin began the First Five-Year Plan
- 1934-1938, Stalin's Great Purge began and escalated
- 1940-1980, Cold War years
- 1941, Nazi Germany invaded Soviet Union
- 1951, October 4 Sputnik I, first man-made satellite, was launched into orbit from Russia
- 1953, Stalin dies, replaced by Nikita Khrushchev
- 1953, Lunik III launched, took first pictures of back, or "dark side", of the moon
- 1955, Summits began between leaders of USSR, USA, France, and Britain
- 1957, November 3 Sputnik II launched with dog named Laika, first living creature to travel in space
- 1967, Russian spacecraft landed on Venus
- 1968, Soviet Army invaded Czechoslovakia
- 1972, SALT 1 was signed
- 1979, SALT 2 was signed
- 1979, Russian-Afghanistan War began
- 1980, US boycotted Olympic Games in Moscow
- 1985, Mikhail Gorbachev became leader of USSR
- 1988, Communist Party initiated political reform
- 1991, Mikhail Gorbachev resigned and all fifteen republics declared independence
- 1991, Boris Yeltsin became president of Russia
- 2000, Vladimir Putin became president of Russia
- 2002, violence in Chechnya escalates
- 2004, Putin wins second term

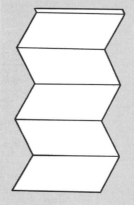

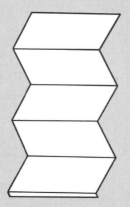

Time Line

China, Taiwan, and Mongolia

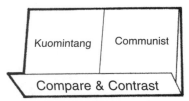

Kuomintang | Communist

Compare & Contrast

Two-tab matchbook

WHO:
Dalai Lama

WHAT:

WHEN:

WHERE:

Four-door book

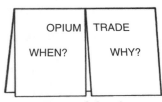

OPIUM | TRADE

WHEN? | WHY?

Two-tab book

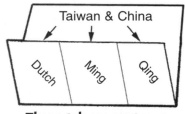

Taiwan & China

Dutch | Ming | Qing

Three-tab concept map

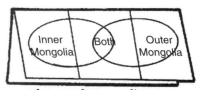

Inner Mongolia | Both | Outer Mongolia

Three-tab Venn diagram

Skill	Activity Suggestion	Foldable Parts
locate	the following countries and their capital cities on a world map: • China, Beijing • Taiwan, Taipei • Mongolia, Ulaanbaatar	any number
K-LK-L	ask yourself what you know, what you would like to know, and review what you learn about	3
list	information about each country in this area and determine what they have in common	3
compare and contrast	the Kuomintang (KMT) led by Chiang Kai-shek, (leader of the party after the death of KMT founder Sun Yat-sen) and the Communist movement led by Mao Zedong	2
investigate	the who, what, when, where for the following: • Sun Yat-Sen, 1911 revolution in China • Mao Zedong, China • Jiang-Jieshi, Taiwan • Dalai Lama, Tibet • Yumzhagiyen Tsedenbal, Mongolia, 1952-1984	4
investigate	the what, when, where, why/how for the following: • giant panda • Treaty of Nanking, 1841-1842 • Kuomintang, or Nationalist Party • Three Gorges Dam, China • Naadam Festival, Mongolia • the Cultural Revolution, 1965	4
research	and report on when and why China was forced to accept trade in opium (previously banned)	2
describe	China before and after ports were opened to trade	2
locate	the following geographic locations and understand their importance to the area: • Plateau of Tibet, average height 13,000 ft	1
	• Gobi Desert and Taklimakan Desert	2
	• East China Sea and South China Sea	2
	• Manchurian Plain and North China Plain • Yangtze, Yellow, Xi Rivers	2 3
	• Ring of Fire	1
outline	the history of Taiwan and its relationship with China: • Dutch in Taiwan • Taiwan as a Ming enclave • Taiwan under Qing rule	3
make a Venn diagram	and use it to compare and contrast "Inner Mongolia" and the country of Mongolia, formerly called "Outer Mongolia"	3
debate	the pros and cons of the 1993 government ban on satellite dishes	2
speculate	as to the political, economic, and social impact of the 2008 Olympics	3
show cause and effect	of the Tiananmen Square Protest of 1989	2
examine	the past, present, and future of each country	3

China, Taiwan, and Mongolia

Make a time line of some of the key historic events taking place in this region since 1800:

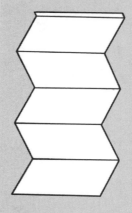

- 1839, First Opium War began in China
- 1841-1842, Britain took Hong Kong from China, Hong Kong became richest trading post in the region
- 1842, Treaty of Nanking
- 1856-1860, Second Opium War
- 1860, two ports on Taiwan's western coast opened to foreign ships
- 1899, secret society of Chinese, called Boxers, rose against Christian missionaries in China
- 1899, Aurel Stein, archeologist who spent his life searching for the ancient Silk Road which crossed the Gobi Desert and was traveled by caravans carrying silk to Europe and ports of trade, began his life's work
- 1900-1901, Boxer Rebellion
- 1911, revolution led by Dr. Sun Yat-sen
- 1912, emperor P'u-i abdicated and China became a republic
- 1915, Yuan Shi-k'ai declared himself emperor
- 1920's, central government broke down and power was held by 'Warlords' until they were defeated by Jiang-Jieshi
- 1921, Chinese Communist Party was formed
- 1923, Nationalists and Communists formed an alliance and opposed warlords and imperialism in China
- 1924, Mongolia gained independence from China, became communist with Soviet Union
- 1933, Communists began "Long March" to Shensi
- 1945, Japan defeated, Taiwan and the P'enghu Islands were given back to China
- 1949, Taiwan became a free society
- 1949, December 8: Chiang moved the KMT government from Nanjing to Taipei as communists took control of China
- 1950, China took Tibet
- 1950, Communist plans to invade Taiwan averted when the US sent naval forces to defend the island
- 1954 Chiang Kai-shek was reelected president of the Republic of China while in Taiwan
- 1954, US agreed to protect Taiwan from China
- 1957, 'Great Leap Forward'
- 1965, Chairman Mao's Cultural Revolution began
- 1970s China banned most outside communication
- 1972, US president Richard Nixon visited Beijing
- 1978, China allowed free enterprise
- 1979, the United States formalized relations with mainland China and ended diplomatic ties to Taiwan
- 1980, 1954 US-Taiwan defense treaty of lapsed
- 1989, Tiananmen Square
- 1990, Mongolia became a democracy
- 1990s, reforms brought economic growth
- 1994, China began Three Georges Dam
- 1997, China regained city of Hong Kong from UK
- 1999, China regained city of Macau from Portugal
- 2001, China became a member of the WTO
- 2003, March: Hu Jintao elected President replacing Jiang Zemin
- 2003, China launched its first manned spacecraft

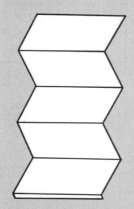

Time Line

India, Pakistan, and Kashmir

India	Pakistan	Kashmir

1x3 Chart

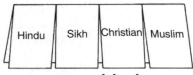

Four-tab book

Hindu | Sikh | Christian | Muslim

Taj Mahal

Picture-frame book

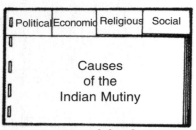

Political | Economic | Religious | Social

Causes
of the
Indian Mutiny

Top-tab book

Key Events in Pak-
istan s History

| East & West Pakistan |
| 1st Indo-Pakistan War |
| 2nd Indo-Pakistan War |
| Bangladesh |
| Nuclear Testing & Ceasfire |

**Layer book
(3 sheets of paper)**

list	information about each country in this area and determine what they have in common: • India • Pakistan • Kashmir	3
locate	the following on a map: • Karakoram Mountain Range • Himalaya Mountain Range • Islamabad, Pakistan • New Deli, India	any number
K-LK-L	ask yourself what you know, what you would like to know, and review what you learn about the history of India	3
chart	information on each of the following religions and describe their past and present influences: Hindu, Sikh, Christian, and Muslim	4
investigate	the who, what, when, where for the following: • Shah Jahan, builder of Taj Mahal • Mohandas Gandhi • M.A. Jinnah, Muslim League • Benazir Bhutto	4
	the what, when, where, why/how for the following: • East India Company • green revolution • reincarnation • Diwali, holiday • Taj Mahal in Agra, India	4
locate	the following geographic locations and understand their importance to the area: • Pakistan • Kashmir • Himalayan Mountains	4
sequence	seven key events in the history of India: • "India Mutiny" • British governments takes control of India • Ghandi's March to the Sea • Bengal Famine • India and Pakistan become independent • Indo-Pakistan War • India and Pakistan restore diplomatic ties	7
	five key events in the history of Pakistan: • East and West Pakistan established • India and Pakistan fight over Kashmir • Second war between India and Pakistan • East Pakistan secedes and becomes Bangladesh • Potential war at border and eventual Kashmir ceasefire	5
list	arguments for and against Kashmir being divided between India and Pakistan in 1947	2
make a Venn diagram	and use it to compare the Indian-controlled region and the Pakistan controlled region of Kashmir	3
show cause and effect	of outsourcing	2
	of "War on Terror"	2
examine	the past, present, and future of the economic status of each country	3

India, Pakistan, and Kashmir

Make a time line of some of the key historic events taking place in this region since 1850:

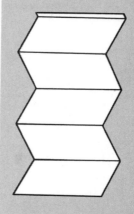

- 1853, first railroads and telegraph systems in India
- 1857, "Indian Mutiny", revolt against East India Co. which started India on the road to nationalism
- 1858, British government took control of the government of India
- 1860-1880, several nationalist movements began
- 1885, Indian National Congress founded and led the fight for India's independence
- 1912, construction began on New Delhi, India's beautifully planned capital city
- 1915, Mohandas Gandhi became leader of Congress Party and began peaceful civil disobedience to force British out of India
- 1930, March to the Sea, led by Gandhi
- 1930-1932, Round Table Conferences in London
- 1935, Government of India Act allowed Indians to play a major part in their own government
- 1943, Bengal Famine
- 1945, WWII ended and M.A. Jinnah, leader of Muslim League, called for a separate Muslim state called Pakistan
- 1947, India and Pakistan became independent and a lingering dispute began over Kashmir in the north
- 1947, Jawaharlal Nehru, first prime minister
- 1965, the Indo-Pakistan (Bangladesh) War
- 1966, Tashkent Agreement, India and Pakistan
- 1966, Indira Gandhi led India
- 1971, East Pakistan became a nation, Bangladesh
- 1984, Indira Gandhi, prime minister, assassinated, son Rajiv Gandhi becomes prime minister
- 1987, Gandhi sent Indian troops to Sri Lanka to suppress a rebellion by Tamil guerrillas
- 1988, Gandhi, was the first prime minister to visit Pakistan in nearly 25 years
- 1990, India's finances were badly hit when Iraq invaded Kuwait
- 1991, Rajiv Gandhi, prime minister, assassinated by a Sri Lankin Tamil guerrilla terrorist
- 1991, P. V. Narasimha Rao, new prime minister
- 1991-1996, economic stimuli and growth
- 1996 elections began a period of unrest in India, resulting in wariness by foreign investors
- 1997, Rao indicted for corruption
- 1998, new prime minister Vajpayee
- 1998, new government tests five nuclear devices in underground detonations and Pakistan responded with its own nuclear tests
- 2000, India created three new states—Uttaranchal from Uttar Pradesh, Chhattisgarh from Madhya Pradesh, and Jharkhand from Bihar
- 2001, earthquake struck India's Gujarat state which resulted in about 20,000 deaths and great destruction
- 2003, India and Pakistan restored full diplomatic ties
- 2004, December 26: the Asian Tsunami hits South India, killing thousands

Time Line

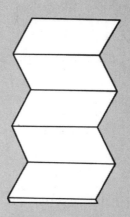

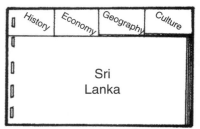

Top-tab book

**Layer book
(3 sheets of paper)**

Pyramid fold

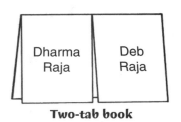

Two-tab book

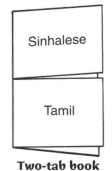

Two-tab book

South Asia

Skill	Activity Suggestion	Foldable Parts
locate	the following countries and their capital cities on a world map: • India, New Deli • Pakistan, Islamabad • Kashmir, Srinagar • Bangladesh, Dhaka • Nepal, Kathmandu • Bhutan, Thimphu • Sri Lanka, Kotte • Maldives, Malè	any number
K-LK-L	ask yourself what you know, what you would like to know, and review what you learn about this region	3
chart	information about each country in this area and determine what they have in common	8
investigate	the who, what, when, where for the following: • Siddartha Gautama, the Buddha • Sheikh Mujibur Rahman • King Jigme Singye Wangchuck • Sinhalese and Tamils (Sri Lanka)	4
	the what, when, where, why/how for the following: • Sepoy Rebellion • dagobas • batheli boats • Poya Day	4
locate	the following geographic locations and understand their importance to the area: • Ganges River • Khyber Pass and the Hindu Kush Mountains • Bay of Bengal • Mount Everest, Nepal	1
research	the dual system of government used in Bhutan until 1907--a spiritual leader entitled "dharma raja" and a civil government leader entitled "deb raja"	2
outline	the reigns of the hereditary druk gyalpos of Bhutan since 1907: • Ugyen Wangchuck, 1907 and 1926 • Jigme Wangchuck, 1926 to 1952 • Jigme Dorji Wangchuck, 1952 to 1972 • Jigme Dorji Wangchuck, 1972-	4
discuss	Bhutan's decision to close the Nepal border and leave open the India border	2
	India's airlifting of supplies to the Tamils which caused tension between India and Sri Lanka	2
compare	the views of the Sinhalese and the Tamil	2
make a timeline	of the unbroken line of Sultans who ruled the Maldives from 1153-1953	any number

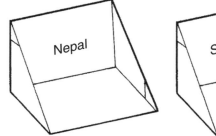

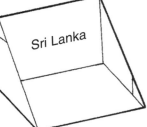

South Asia

Make a time line of some of the key historic events taking place in this region since 1800:

- 1616, Bhutan's theocratic government founded by a Drukpa monk, Ngawang Namgyal, who became the leader of united Bhutan
- 1616-1907, duel government--civil and spiritual--existed in Bhutan for nearly 300 years
- 1887, Maldives Islands became a British protectorate
- 1857-1859, Nepal aided Britain, Sepoy Rebellion
- 1914-1918, World War I
- 1923, British government reaffirmed Nepal's independence through a treaty
- 1939-1945, Nepal aided Allies with Gurkha soldiers
- 1939-1945, Sri Lanka was used as an Allied base of operations in the offensive against Japan
- 1947, Ceylon Independence Act
- 1948, Ceylon became independent (Sri Lanka)
- 1949, Treaty of Peace and Friendship signed by Bhutan and India
- 1948, February 4 Ceylon independent dominion within the British Commonwealth of Nations
- 1948, Nepal and US established diplomatic relations
- 1947-1971, Bangladesh was a province of Pakistan
- 1951, Ceylon minister of local government, Solomon Bandaranaike, resigned from the cabinet and formed his own party, the Sri Lanka Freedom Party (SLFP)
- 1955, Bangladesh called "East Pakistan"
- 1958, SLFP-led government passed the Official Language Act--Sinhala only official language
- 1965, the Maldives independent as sultanate
- 1968, people of Maldives voted to be a republic
- 1971, leaders of "East Pakistan" declared the province independent and called it Bangladesh
- 1971, December 16 Pakistani troops surrendered to Bangladeshi and Indian troops
- 1972, new constitution ratified and Ceylon's name changed to Sri Lanka, and its status changed from a dominion to a republic
- 1972, Ceylon officially changed name to Sri Lanka
- 1983, bloody battle began between two major groups in Sri Lanka--Sinhalese and Tamils
- 1987, an Indian peacekeeping force replaced Sri Lankan troops in the Jaffna Peninsula
- 1988, Indian troops foiled a coup attempt by Tamil mercenaries in Maldives
- 1998 Maldives adopted a new constitution.
- 1990, Nepal adopted new constitution providing for a multiparty system
- 1990, all Indian troops withdrawn from Sri Lanka
- 1996, Bangladesh and India reached an agreement to share the waters of the Ganges
- 2001, King Birendra and eight royal family members were fatally shot in the royal palace in Kathmandu, by Crown Prince Dipendra, who also shot himself

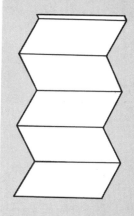

Time Line

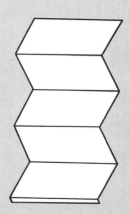

Middle East

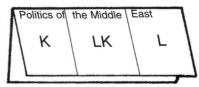

Three-tab book

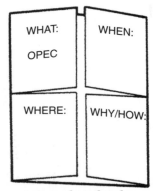

Four-door book

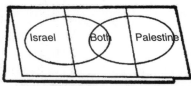

Three-tab Venn diagram

Layer book
(2 sheets of paper)

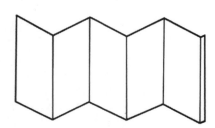

Timeline:
Events of the Six Day War

locate	the following countries and their capital cities on a world map: • Bahrain, Manama • Cyprus, Nicosia • Iran, Tehran • Iraq, Baghdad • Israel, Jerusalem • Israeli-occupied Gaza Strip and West Bank • Jordan, Amman • Kuwait, Kuwait • Lebanon, Beirut • Oman, Muscat • Qatar, Doha • Saudi Arabia, Riyadh • Syria, Damascus • Turkey, Ankara • the United Arab Emirates, Abu Dhabi • Yemen, Sanaa • and the African country of Egypt, Cairo	any number
K-LK-L	ask yourself what you know, what you would like to know, and review what you learn about the politics of the Middle East	3
chart	information about 5 countries in this area and determine what they have in common	5
investigate	the who, what, when, where for the following: • David Ben-Gurion, Israel • Gamal Abdel Nasser, Egypt • Anwar el-Sadat, Egypt • Yasser Arafat, PNA	4
	the what, when, where, why/how for the following: • Palestinian Refugee Camps • Organization of Petroleum Exploring Countries, OPEC, 1960 • *intifida*, "uprising"	4
locate	the following geographic locations and understand their importance to the area: • Jerusalem • Persian Gulf • Suez Canal	2
make a Venn diagram	to compare and contrast the following countries: • Iran and Iraq • Israel and Palestine	3
research	why 1948 Palestine was divided into two states: • an Arab state • a Jewish state	2
outline	three or more changes that took place in the Middle East after WWII: • Syria, gained independence • Lebanon, gained independence • Jordan, total self rule	3
determine	why both Jews and Arabs claim the land of Palestine	2
sequence	events of the 1967, Six-Day War; Israel mounts air strikes against Egypt, 1) broke blockade, 2) occupied Sinai Peninsula, 3)took land on the West Bank of Jordan River, 4) occupied Jerusalem, and 5) took control of Golan Heights	5

Middle East

Make a time line of some of the key historic events taking place in this region since 1800:

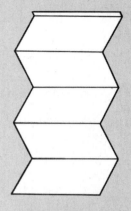

- 1912, October 8 The First Balkan War, against Turkey, began eventually leading to WWI
- 1946, France left Syria and Lebanon; Britain granted independence to Jordan
- 1948, UN divided Palestine into a Jewish state (Israel) and an Arab state (Palestine), Britain withdraws
- 1948, May 14 Israel declared statehood
- 1951, July 20 King Abdullah of Jordan, assassinated
- 1956, Suez War began, Nassar seized Suez Canal Co.
- 1960, Organization of Petroleum Exploring Countries, OPEC formed
- 1964, Palestine Liberation Organization formed by Egypt with Yasser Arafat
- 1967, Nassar blockaded Israel shipping
- 1967, the Six-Day War
- 1970, Nassar died replaced by Anwar el-Sadat
- 1972, September 5 Olympic Games, Munich Arab terrorists took Israeli athletes hostage
- 1973, Arab-Israeli War, Yom Kippur War
- 1975, border settlement between Iraq and Iran
- 1979, Israel and Egypt signed Camp David Accords
- 1979, Shah Mohammed Reza Puhlavi left Iran, the Ayatollah Khomeini returned from exile, and made Iran an Islamic republic
- 1980, Iraqi president Saddam Hussein invaded Iran
- 1981, Iran freed 52 Americans taken hostage when they seized the American embassy during the Iran revolution in 1979
- 1981, October 6 President Sadat of Egypt was assassinated by Muslim extremists at a military parade on the eighth anniversary of the Arab-Israeli War
- 1988, cease-fire agreement between Iraq and Iran reached with help of United Nations
- 1990, Iraq's President Saddam Hussein invaded and annexed Kuwait leading to Gulf War
- 1991, January 15 deadline for Hussein to withdraw from Kuwait
- 1991, Gulf War
- 1993, August 20 Oslo Accords signed in an attempt to bring peace between the PLO and the state of Israel
- 2001, International coalition entered Afghanistan in pursuit of al-Qaeda, believed to be responsible for the September 11 attacks in the U.S.
- 2002, UN weapons inspectors returned to Iraq for the first time in almost four years
- 2003, March 19 U.S. declared war on Iraq
- 2003, December 13 Hussein is captured by U.S. troops
- 2004, November 11 Yassar Arafat died of undetermined causes
- 2005, December 15 Iraqis vote to elect members of Iraqi Assembly
- 2006, December 30 Saddam Hussein executed

Time Line

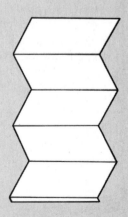

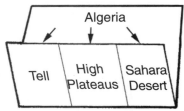

Three-tab concept map

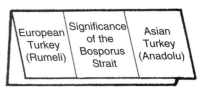

Three-tab book

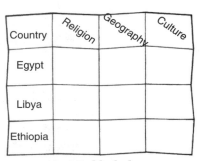

4x4 Folded chart

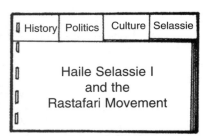

Top-tab book

Four-tab book

North Africa and Southwest Asia

Skill	Activity Suggestion	Foldable Parts
locate	the following countries and their capital cities on a world map: **Northern Africa:** • Algeria, Algiers • Egypt, Cairo • Ethiopia, Addis Ababa • Libya, Tripoli • Mauritania, Nouakchott • Morocco, Rabat • Sudan, Khartoum • Tunisia, Tunis **Southwest Asia:** • Afghanistan, Kabulany • Bahrain, Manama • Cyprus, Nicosia • Iran, Tehran • Iraq, Baghdad • Israel, Tel Aviv/Jerusalem • Jordan, Amman • Kuwait, Kuwait • Lebanon, Beirut • Oman, Muscat • Qatar, Doha • Saudi Arabia, Riyadh • Syria, Damascus • Turkey, Istanbul • United Arab Emirates, Abu Dhabi • Yemen, Sanaa	1
K-LK-L	ask yourself what you know, what you would like to know, and review what you learn about North Africa and Southwest Asia	3
list	information on countries in this area and determine what they have in common: • religion, the most common religion in region • desert land • cultural adaptations to desert life	3
explain	how fossils and rock carvings prove the Sahara was not always a desert	2
investigate	the who, what, when, where for the following: • Berbers • Kurds • Menelik I, son of Queen of Sheba and King Solomon • Haile Selassie I, Ethiopia • Mumammar al-Qaddafi, Libya • Shirin Abadi, Iran	4
	the what, when, where, why/how for the following: • the Suez Canal, between Mediterranean and Red Sea • Aswan High Dam • OPEC, Organization of Petroleum Exporting Countries • the term "Cradle of Humanity"	4
locate	the following geographic locations and understand their importance to the area: • Sahara Desert, Negev Desert, Syrian Desert • Strait of Gibraltar • Nile, Euphrates, Tigris, Jordan River • Dead Sea, Mediterranean Sea, • Golan Heights • Makkah • Persian Gulf • Hindu Kush Mountains and the Khyber Pass	any number
discover	why in 1801, the ruler of Tripoli declared war on the US	1
determine	why and how the French gained control of land between the Mediterranean Sea and the Sahara Desert by 1847	2

North Africa and Southwest Asia

Make a time line of some of the key historic events taking place in this region since 1800:

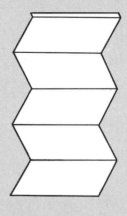

- 1839-1842, first Afghan war between the British in India and the Afghanistan ruler Dost Mohammed Khan
- 1859-1869, building of the Suez Canal
- 1877-1878, Russo-Turkish War
- 1881, Muhammad Ahmed declared himself the Mahdi, or the one who would rid the world of evil, and he launched a holy war against the infidel occupiers of Sudan
- 1884-1885, Khartoum fell to Mahdi's forces and an entire British garrison were massacred
- 1898, British reconquered Sudan
- 1920s-1930s, Kemal Ataturk, Turkey's first president
- 1922, November 4 King Tut's tomb discovered
- 1932, Iraq gained independence as a kingdom
- 1935, Italy invaded Ethiopia
- 1940s, Lebanon became independent from France
- 1946, Jordan became independent from Britain
- 1952-1999, King Hussein I ruled Jordan
- 1956, 'Suez Adventure' began with bombings of Egyptian military targets by an Anglo-French force
- 1962, Algeria gained independence from France
- 1963, Morocco holds first general elections
- 1964, Shah launched campaign to "westernize" Iran which eventually caused an uprising with Islamic clergy and fundamentalists
- 1964, the "October Revolution" established a national government in Sudan
- 1969, Muammar al-Qaddhafi overthrew Libya's king
- 1975-1991, civil war in Lebanon
- 1979, last shah of Iran overthrown, Israel signs peace treaty with Egypt
- 1979, November 4 52 U.S. hostages taken by Islamic militants from the American embassy; released in after 444 days
- 1979, Soviet troops invaded Afghanistan
- 1980-1988, Iran-Iraq war
- 1981, October 6 Egypt's President Anwar al-Sadat was assassinated
- 1985, worst famine in a decade struck Ethiopia; Western countries sent aid
- 1990, Persian Gulf War, Iraq invaded Iran
- 1991, U.S. and USSR both agreed to stop military aid to opposing sides in Afghanistan
- 1992, January 4 state of emergency declared in Algieria as military take-over is lead by Mohamed Boudiaf
- 1994, Israel signed peace treaty with Jordan
- 1996, the Taliban took control of Afghanistan
- 1999, Ethiopia and Eritrea go to war over border dispute
- 1999-2000, Taliban refused to help UN bring Osama bin Laden and al-Queda organization to trial
- 2001, October U.S. and U.K. launch air strikes against Afghanistan
- 2002, President George W. Bush declared Iran, Iraq, and North Korea as the "axis of evil"
- 2001, Taliban driven out of Kabul by US and rebels
- 2004, Darfur crisis in Sudan caused hundreds of thousands of refugees to flee to Chad
- 2004, Free-trade agreement between Morocco and U.S. came into effect
- 2005, December Afghanistan's new parliment began sessions

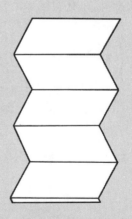

Time Line

Japan and Koreas

Japan | North Korea | South Korea

Japan
and the
Koreas

Top-tab book

Why was Korea called "the Hermit Kingdom"?

Three-quarter book

North
Korea

South
Korea

Two-tab book

Japanese Social Classes
Emperor
Shogun
Daimyo
Samurai
Ronin
Farmers
Outcasts (Eta)

**Layered book
(4 sheets of paper)**

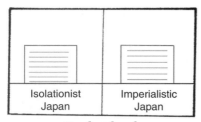

Isolationist Japan | Imperialistic Japan

Pocket book

Skill	Activity Suggestion	Foldable Parts

locate	the following on a world map:
	• Japan, Tokyo
	   largest islands in the archipelago
	      Honshu
	      Hokkaido
	      Kyushu
	      Shikoku
	• North Korea, Pyongyang
	• South Korea, Seou
		1

chart	information on each country in this area and determine three things they have in common	3
investigate	the who, what, when, where for the following: • Adams, William (1564-1620), first Englishman in Japan (shipwrecked), he became a Japanese samurai • shoguns of the Tokuwaga family • Kim Il Sung or Kim Jong Il, North Korea	4
explain why and how	the Korea, peninsula in Asia has been divided since 1948 into two political entities: • the Democratic People's Republic of Korea (North) • Republic of Korea (South Korea)	2
investigate	the what, when, where, why/how for the following: • *samurai*--a privileged class skilled in combat • *zaibatsu*--led to nationalism and militarism • Burma--Thailand railroad built by forced labor, 1943 • Japanese slogan--"Asia for the Asiatics." • kamikaze, or "divine wind" • South Korean chaebols	4
locate	the following geographic locations and understand their importance to the area: • Mount Fuji • Kanto Plain, eastern Honshu • Sea of Japan • Korean Peninsula • Yalu River, divides Korea from China	5
investigate	Japan before and after 1854 when it became open to world trade	2
Venn diagram	North Korea, South Korea, both	3
summarize	Commodore Perry's role in Japan's history	1
outline	four key events in the expansion of Japan	4
compare and contrast	how Japan and the United States dealt with the decrease in labor force during WWII: • US used women in factories, agriculture, others • Japan brought in Korean and Chinese laborers	2
describe	past, present, future attitudes towards war	3
search the web	terrorism in Japan	1

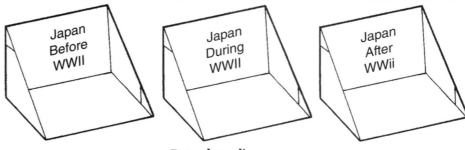

Japan Before WWII | Japan During WWII | Japan After WWii

Four-door dioramas

Japan and Koreas

Make a time line of some of the key historic events taking place in this region since 1800:

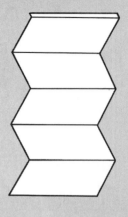

- 1636, Decree of 1636 called for isolation and cut Japan off from outside influences
- 1842, reforms began in Japan
- 1853, US sent Commodore Perry to Japan to demand Japan open its ports to trade
- 1854, Japan ended isolation with Treaty of Kanagawa
- late 1800's, began to use western ideas to modernize
- 1867, Meiji (Matsuhito, 1852-1912), became emperor and wanted to modernize Japan
- 1871, Meiji commanded that all feudal lands be abolished and reforms occurred in education and other areas, such as postal services
- 1872 onward, Germans trained the Japanese army and British trained the Japanese navy
- 1877, Satsuma Rebellion, samurai fought to restore old way of life and their social class, but failed
- early 1900, Japan became military leader of Asia
- 1882, the Bank of Japan was established by this time
- 1891, Japan attacked China
- 1904-1905, Russo-Japanese War, Japan won   • 1905, Japan formally began domination of Korea--Protectorate Treaty
- 1910, Japan formally annexed Korea
- 1910-1919, Japan forced changes in Korea
- 1919, March First Movement, nonviolent Korean demonstrations for independence
- 1930s-1940s, Japan tried to assimilate the Korean population by outlawing Korean language and Korean family names
- 1930s, Japan took land in China
- 1941, December 7: Japan attacked Pearl Harbor
- 1941, December 25: Hong Kong surrendered to Japan
- 1945, August 6: atomic bomb dropped on Hiroshima
- 1945, August 8: Russia declared war on Japan
- 1945, August 9: atomic bomb dropped on Nagasaki
- 1945, August 15: Japan surrendered (V-J Day)
- 1945, Korea liberated from Japanese rule by Allies
- 1947, Korea divided along the 38th parallel
- 1948, U.S.-sponsored elections led to Republic of Korea in the south, and in September the north established the Democratic People's Republic of Korea (DPRK)
- 1950, armies of North Korea invaded South Korea and the Korean war began
- 1951, truce talks began in July of this year
- 1953, Korean War ended, Korea divided along 38th parallel again--no permanent peace settlement
- 2000, leaders of North and South Korea met for first time since division
- 2006, October 9 North Korea announced that it had conducted its first nuclear tests

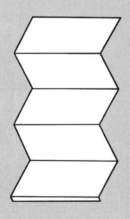

Time Line

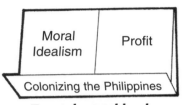

How did Thailand resist colonial rule unlike the rest of Southeast Asia?

Three-quarter book

Moral Idealism | Profit

Colonizing the Philippines

Two-tab matchbook

Indirect Colonial Rule | Direct Colonial Rule

1x2 Chart

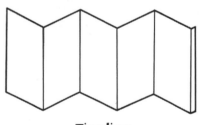

Timeline: Vietnam War

American Attitudes | about the | Vietnam War

Before | During | After

Trifold book

Southeast Asia

Skill	Activity Suggestion	Foldable Parts
locate	the following on a world map: Mainland: • Cambodia (Kampuchea) • Laos • Malaysia • Myanmar, (formerly Burma) • Thailand • Vietnam Island Countries: • Brunei • Indonesia • the Philippines • Singapore	any number
chart	information about the countries in this area and determine three or more things they have in common: • monsoons • Colonial rule (exception of Thailand) • civil war	3+
investigate	the who, what, when, where for the following: • Ho Chi Minh, Vietnam • King Monkut, Thailand • Pol Pot, Cambodia • Ferdinand Marcos, Philippines	4
	the what, when, where, why/how for the following: • temple of Angkor Wat, Cambodia, 1100's • Khmer Rouge, Cambodia • Pagodas at Pagan, Myanmar	4
locate	the following geographic locations and understand their importance to the area: • Malay Peninsula • Gulf of Tonkin • Celebes, Java, South China, and Philippine Sea • Indian Ocean	any number
determine	the past and present importance of spice trade to the region	2
outline	what led to the division of Vietnam into North and South Vietnam, and some of the problems that resulted	2
research	how the United States gained control of the Philippines at the end of the Spanish-American War, and how the Philippines became a democratic republic in 1946	2
describe	attitudes of Americans towards the Vietnam War before, during, and after the war	3
	how Singapore can be one of the world's smallest countries, but have one of the world's strongest economies	1
debate	pros and cons of Singapore's strict law and punishment codes	2

Southeast Asia

Make a time line of some of the key historic events taking place in this region since 1800:

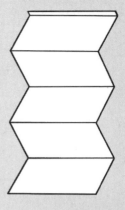

- 1898, Philippines became US territory after 300 years as a Spanish colony
- 1945, Vietnam, Cambodia (Kampuchea) and Laos occupied by Japanese during WWII
- 1945, Communist leader Ho Chi Minh and his Viet declared Vietnam independent in 1945
- 1946, Philippines became independent
- 1947, fighting between French and Viet Minh, with Americans aiding the French and Emperor Bao Dai
- 1949, Indonesian independence from Dutch
- 1953, Cambodia free of French rule
- 1953, America paying for 80% of France's war
- 1954, French defeated at Dien Bien Phu, withdraw
- 1954, Geneva agreement; five years of peace
- 1959, unrest escalated--North and South Vietnam
- 1960s, Vietnam War
- 1964, Tonkin Gulf Incident
- 1965, Singapore independent of British rule
- 1968, Tet offensive
- 1967, Muda Hassanal Bolkiah became the twenty-ninth sultan of Brunei
- 1969-1971, Pol Pot took over Cambodia, nearly 2 million people were killed or died from persecution
- 1973, US withdrew from Vietnam war with signing of Paris Peace Treaty
- 1974, North Vietnam breached cease-fire agreement
- 1975, Cambodia freed of French rule
- 1975 ,Communist Khmer Rouge in Cambodia
- 1975-1976, South Vietnam was captured by communists, the war ended, and Vietnam was reunited as the Socialist Republic of Vietnam
- 1984, Brunei's independence from United Kingdom
- 1986, People Power Movement toppled Marcos regime in Philippines
- 1989, Burma became Myanmar, name changed by the military government that took over in 1988 (Yangon, formerly Rangoon, was designated capital)
- 1989, Laos held first National Assembly elections
- 1993, Cambodia brought back its king
- 1997, Indonesia faced economic crisis, resignation of President Suharto
- 1999, democratic elections held in Indonesia
- 2003, Abdullah bin Ahmad Badawi became Malaysia's prime minister and leader of UMNO.

Time Line

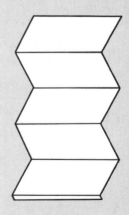

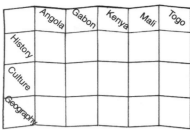

6x4 Folded chart

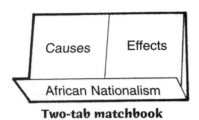

Two-tab matchbook

Causes | Effects

African Nationalism

Segregation in the United States | Apartheid in South Africa

Two-tab book

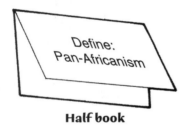

Define: Pan-Africanism

Half book

| British | French | German | Italian |

4x1 Folded chart

Africa

Skill	Activity Suggestion	Foldable Parts
locate	the following on a world map: • Angola • Madagascar • Benin • Malawi • Botswana • Mali • Burkina Faso • Maurintania • Burundi • Mauritius • Cameroon • Mozambique • Cape Verde • Namibia • Central African Republic • Niger • Chad • Nigeria • Comoros • Rwanda • Congo • Sao Tome and Principe • Congo, • Senegal Democratic Republic of the • Seychelles • Cote d'Ivoire • Sierra Leone • Djibouti • Somalia • Equatorial Guinea • South Africa • Eritrea • Sudan • Ethiopia • Swaziland • Gabon • Tanzania • Gambia • Togo • Ghana • Uganda • Guinea • Zambia • Guinea-Bissau • Zimbabwe • Kenya • Lesotho • Liberia	any number
design a table and collect	information on 5 or more countries in this area, and determine what they have in common: • most were colonies of other countries at one time • civil wars plague many African countries	5+
investigate	the who, what, when, where for the following: • Chaka, founded Zulu Empire • David Livingston, explorer • Jomo Kenyatta, Kenya • Kwane Nkrumah, Ghana • Desmond Tutu, South Africa • Nelson Mandela, South Africa	4
	the what, when, where, why/how for the following: • Pan-Africanism • apartheid • eco-tourists • Lost Boys of Sudan • AIDS in Africa and/or tsetse fly in Africa • Great Mosque of Djenne	4
locate	the following geographic locations and understand their importance to the area: • Mount Kilimanjaro	1
	• Great Rift Valley	1
	• Serengeti Plain	1
	• Horn of Africa and Cape of Good Hope	2
	• important lakes: Lake Tanganyika, Lake Volta, Lake Malawi	3+
	• Gulf of Guinea	1
	• Namib Desert, Kalahari Desert	2
	• Zambezi River and Victoria Falls	2
chart	the African countries controlled by each of the following empires: British, French, German, Italian	4
determine	the cultural impact of WWI on Africans	1
compare	the political status of Africa before and after WWI	2
	the political status of Africa before and after WWII	2

Africa

Make a time line of some of the key historic events taking place in this region since 1800:

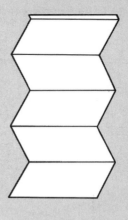

- 1818, Zulu Empire founded by Chaka (d.1828)
- 1822, Liberia founded by freed American slaves
- 1835-1837, Great Trek by Afrikaners in South Africa
- 1847, Liberia became the first African colony to become independent
- 1852-1856, Livingston crossed Africa
- 1879, Zulu War
- 1884-1885, Berlin conference divided Africa into "spheres of influence"
- 1899-1902, Boer War (Dutch settlers called Boers)
- 1912, Apartheid, set up in South Africa
- 1918, Kenya was made British colony after WWI
- 1930, mouth of Niger River discovered opening Africa
- 1935, Abyssinia (Ethiopia) attacked by Italy
- 1938, "extinct" coelacanth caught off South Africa
- 1948, South Africa imposed apartheid laws and became a republic
- 1956, France left Morocco and Tunisia
- 1957, Ghana became first African nation to gain independence
- 1958, France withdrew from Guinea
- 1960, Mobutu became ruler of newly named Zaire
- 1960, independence from France for Mauritania, Mali, Burkina Faso, Niger, and Chad
- 1960s, anti-apartheid sentiments grew as world views (especially western) became more liberal
- 1960s, civil war in Nigeria
- 1961, crisis in the Congo
- 1962, France withdrew from Cameroon, Congo, Gabon, Chad, Central African Republic, Algeria
- 1962, Nelson Mandela imprisoned
- 1963, Organization of African Unity was formed
- 1963, Kenya won independence
- 1965, minority white Rhodesians declared independence and excluded blacks from government
- 1966, South African prime minister stabbed to death in Parliament, Cape Town
- 1967, first human heart-transplant operation, Cape Town
- 1967, Civil War in Nigeria
- 1971, Idi Amin seized control of Uganda
- 1975, Angola independent from Portugal
- 1980s, terrible drought in West African countries, and then in Ethiopia, Somalia, and Sudan
- 1980s-1990's, civil war in Mozambique
- 1989, Nobel Prize for literature--Chinua Achebe
- 1989-1996, civil war in Liberia
- 1990, Namibia independent from Republic of South Africa
- 1990s, Hutu and Tutsi fighting, genocide in Rwanda
- 1990s AIDS infections escalated to an epidemic
- 1994, Nelson Mandela elected president of South Africa
- 1994, the presidents of Rwanda and Burundi both killed in an airplane crash--Huto and Tutsi genocides
- 1997, Zaire back to Democratic Republic of Congo
- 1999, free elections in Nigeria
- 2001, the Organisation for African Unity is replaced by the African Union
- 2002, failed coup leads to Ivory Coast civil war
- 2004, genocide begins in Darfur
- 2005, leaders of the 8 largest economies in the world pledge to double aid to Africa by 2010

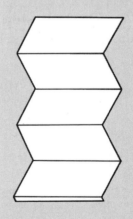

Time Line

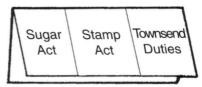

Three-tab book

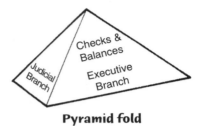

Pyramid fold

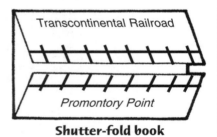

Two-tab matchbook

Shutter-fold book

Layer book
(2 sheets of paper)

United States

Skill	Activity Suggestion	Foldable Parts
research	and report on the following: • the Seven Years War, 1755 • the Treaty of Paris • the Boston Tea Party	3
describe	each of the following acts and/or duties levied by the British to pay debts: • the Sugar Act, 1764 • the Stamp Act, 1765 • the Townsend Duties, 1767	3
cause and effect	of the Declaration of Independence	2
read	and describe how the Declaration of Independence impacts your life today	1
determine	how the constitution of the United States protected and provided for both state and federal governments	2
compare and and contrast	presidents, dictators, and royalty	3
	the American Revolution and the French Revolution	2
list	three reasons Americans choose to have a president	3
explain	the system of checks and balances developed to prevent a president from acting dictatorially	1
chart	information about each geographic region of the US comparing and contrasting the following: population distribution, products and resources, climate	any number
make a time line	outlining major events in the eradication of and/or the forcing of Native Americans to move further and further west	any number
investigate	the who, what, when, where for the following: • George Washington • Chief Joseph • John F. Kennedy • Dr. Martin Luther King, Jr.	4
	the what, when, where, why/how for the following: • White House • Transcontinental Railroad • Statue of Liberty, Ellis Island, Angel Island • St. Louis Arch • Golden Gate Bridge	4
locate	the following geographic locations and understand their importance to the country: • Great Lakes • Great Salt Lake • Gulf of Mexico • Mississippi, Missouri, Colorado, Ohio Rivers • Rocky, Appalachian, Sierra Nevada Mountains • Death Valley • Grand Canyon • Basin Desert, Mojave Desert, Sonoran Desert, Chihuahuan Desert	any number
determine and explain	how three other countries view the United States	3
research and report on	the position of the United States regarding the following issues: • human rights • democracy • terrorism	3
locate	the following physical geographic regions in the contiguous states of the United States: • Coastal Plains • Appalachian Mountains • Interior Plains • Mountains and Basins • Pacific Coast	5
locate and describe	the physical geography of Alaska and Hawaii	2

United States

Make a time line of some of the key historic events taking place in this region since 1750:

- 1750, Horace Greely wrote "Go west, young man and grow up with the country!"
- 1754-1763, French and Indian War
- 1774, First Continental Congress
- 1775-1783, American Revolutionary War
- 1776, Declaration of Independence signed
- 1787, The Constitution of United States written
- 1789, George Washington inaugurated
- 1791, Bill of Rights ratified
- 1793, Fugitive Slave Act passed
- 1803, Louisiana Purchase
- 1812-1814, War of 1812, US and Britain
- 1814, Francis Scott Key wrote America's national anthem,"The Star-Spangled Banner", during British bombardment of Fort McHenry, Baltimore
- 1826, July 4 Presidents John Adams and Thomas Jefferson died on 50th anniversary of signing of Declaration of Independence
- 1846-1848, War with Mexico
- 1848, gold discovered in California; 1849, gold rush
- 1859, John Brown, anti-slavery activist, was hanged
- 1861-1865, Civil War
- 1663, January 1 Emancipation Proclamation
- 1863, July 3 three day battle of Battle of Gettysburg ended with 37,000 Americans dead or wounded
- 1863, November 19 Lincoln's Gettysburg address
- 1869, railroad tracks met at Promontory, Utah
- 1881, October 26 "Gunfight at the OK Corral"
- 1890, most native Americans were living on reservations
- 1877, Thomas Edison made first sound recording
- 1885, Chicago "gives birth to the skyscraper"
- 1903, December Orville Wright made first flight
- 1917, U.S. entered WWI
- 1920s, the 'Roaring Twenties'
- 1927, first "talkie" movie, The Jazz Singer
- 1929, October 29 US stock market crashed, Great Depression began
- 1932, President Roosevelt's New Deal
- 1933, prohibition repealed after thirteen years
- 1935, Will Rogers, humorist, killed in plane crash
- 1941, Japanese attack Pearl Harbor, US entered WWII
- 1945, end of WWII and Cold War began
- 1947, Truman Doctrine and Marshall Plan
- 1950-1953, U.S. sent troops to back South Korea in the Korean War
- 1954, Civil Rights movement began
- 1960s, noted for protests and liberation movements
- 1962, Cuban missile crisis
- 1963, November 22 Kennedy assassinated in Dallas
- 1965-1973, U.S. combat troops involved in Vietnam War
- 1969, July 20 Neil Armstrong and "Buzz" Aldrin landed on the moon
- 1970s, Equal Pay and Sex Discrimination Acts
- 1974, August 9 Richard Nixon, first US president to resign from office
- 1977, August 16 Elvis Presley, "king of rock", died
- 1987, INF treaty signed
- 1991, Persian Gulf War
- 1994, North American Free Trade Agreement-NAFTA
- 2001, September 11 terrorists attacked World Trade Center and the Pentagon
- 2001, U.S. and Britain led coalition invaded Afghanistan
- 2003, U.S. and Britain led coalition invaded and occupied Iraq
- 2006, Hurrican Katrina became the costliest and one of the deadliest storms in U.S. history

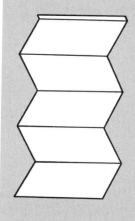

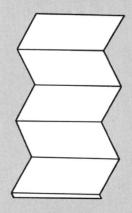

Time Line

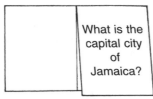

Three-quarter book

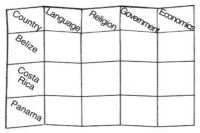

5x4 Chart

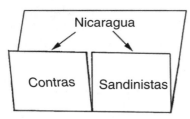

Military Rule	Civilian Rule

1x2 Chart

Nicaragua → Contras / Sandinistas

Two-tab concept map

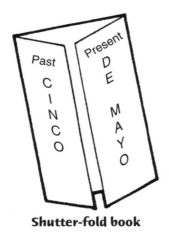

Shutter-fold book

Mexico, Central America, West Indies

locate	the following countries and their capital cities on a world map: • Mexico, Mexico (Distrito Federal) Central America: • Belize, Belmopan • Costa Rica, San Jose • El Salvador, San Salvador • Guatemala, Guatemala • Honduras, Tegucigalpa • Nicaragua, Managua • Panama, Panama West Indies: • Antigua and Barbuda, Saint John's • Bahamas, Nassau • Barbados, Bridgetown • Cuba, Havana • Dominica, Roseau West Indies: • Dominican Republic, Santo Domingo • Grenda, St. George's • Haiti, Port-Au-Prince • Jamaica, Kingston • Puerto Rico, San Juan • St. Kitts and Nevis, Basseterre • St. Lucia, Castries • St. Vincent and the Grenadines, Kingstown • Trinidad and Tobago, Port-Of-Spain	any number
chart	information about the countries in this area and determine what they have in common: • language • religion • government • economics	4
investigate	the who, what, when, where for the following: • Fulgencio Batista, Cuba • Fidel Castro, Cuba • Francisco "Pancho" Villa, Mexico • Diego Rivera and Frida Kahlo, Mexico • Vicente Fox, Mexico • Toussaint-Louverture, Haiti • Manuel Noriega, Panama • Rigoberta Menchu, Guatemala	4
	the what, when, where, why/how for the following: • Independence Day, September 16 • Cinco De Mayo, May 5 • Panama Canal, 1880-1914 • Cuban Missile Crisis, 1962	4
locate	the following geographic locations and understand their importance to the area: • Sierra Madre, three mountain ranges • Yucatan Peninsula • Caribbean Sea • Baja California • Popocatepetl Volcano, "El Popo" • Isthmus of Panama	2
compare	Mexico City to two other large world cities	3
describe	the geographic and political impact of the West Indies forming a 2,000 mile-long breakwater separating the Atlantic Ocean from the Caribbean Sea	2
compare	Pancho Villa, Emiliano Zapata, and Venustiano Carranza	3
celebrate	Cinco de Mayo and explain its significance--past and present	2

Mexico, Central America, West Indies

Make a time line of some of the key historic events taking place in this region since 1800:

- 1801, Toussaint Louverture led slave uprising, and abolished slavery in Haiti
- 1821, Mexico's independence from Spain
- 1898, sinking of US battleship *Maine* in Havana
- 1898, U.S. began control of Puerto Rico
- 1910, Emiliano Zapata led revolution
- 1914-1920, Venustiano Carranza, president, Mexico
- 1917, new constitution for Mexico
- 1938, foreign-owned oil companies refused to pay workers a set wage and the Mexican government nationalized foreign oil companies property-- Petróleos Mexicanos (Pemex) formed
- 1838, Slavery abolished in Jamaica
- 1942, Mexico declared war on the Axis powers
- 1952, Puerto Rico becomes a commonwealth of U.S.
- 1956, Francois Duvalier led military coup and declares himself "president for life" of Haiti
- 1959, Cuban President Batista overthrown by Castro
- 1960, US began trade embargo prohibiting trade with Cuba
- 1961, US broke diplomatic relations with Cuba
- 1961, Bay of Pigs invasion failed
- 1961, December; Castro declared himself a Marxist
- 1962, Cuban missile Crisis
- 1962, Jamaica became independent within the British Commonwealth
- 1979, Sandinistas, Marxist guerrillas, overthrew the Somoza family (Nicaraguan dictators)
- 1979, military took over El Salvador
- 1982, U.S. backed Nicaraguan Contras clashed with Sandinista government
- 1983, Noriega seized control of Panama
- 1985, earthquake in Mexico City
- 1989, US invaded Panama
- 1990, Jean-Bertrand Astride elected president of Haiti; first free elections in 200 years
- 1990, Mexico City became world's most populous city--twenty million inhabitants
- 1989, Noriega nullified election results in Panama
- 1989, US troops arrested Noriega, democracy returned
- 1990, Sandinistas lost free election
- 1991, After collapse of USSR, Soviet advisors left Cuba
- 1992, civil war ended in El Salvador
- 1994, North American Free Trade Agreement (NAFTA)
- 1994, Chiapas Rebellion in Mexico opposed NAFTA and demanded Indian rights
- 1996, Nicaraguan elections resulted in peaceful transfer
- 1996, Guatemalan government and rebels signed peace agreement, ending 36 year civil war
- 1998, Hurrican Mitch caused mass destruction in Honduras
- 1999, Cuban child refugee, Elian Gonzales, sparked campaign in U.S. to prevent him from returning to his father in Cuba; rejoined his father in June 2000
- 2000, Vicente Fox became president of Mexico
- 2002, Honduras re-established diplomatic ties with Cuba after 45 years
- 2005, Guatemala signed Central America free trade agreement with U.S. causing protests
- 2006, Portia Simpson Miller is elected Jamaica's first female prime minister
- 2006, July 31 Castro delegates his duties as President to his brother Raúl Castro

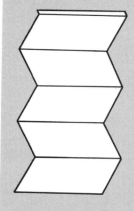

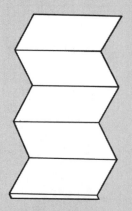

Time Line

Canada

Two-tab book

Canada BEFORE the British North America Act | Canada AFTER the British North America Act

Significance of the Official Languages Act

Half book

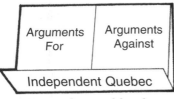

Arguments For | Arguments Against

Independent Quebec

Two-tab matchbook

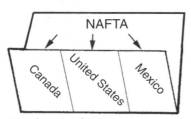

NAFTA

Canada | United States | Mexico

Three-tab concept map

WHAT: The Mounties | WHEN:

Standing cube

locate	the following provinces, territories, and capital cities on a world map: 10 provinces and 3 territories Provinces: • Ontario, Toronto • Quebec, Quebec City • Newfoundland and Labrador, St. Johns • Manitoba, Winnipeg • Saskatchewan, Regina • Alberta, Edmonton • British Columbia • Nova Scotia, Halifax • New Brunswick, Fredericton • Prince Edward Island, Charlottetown Territories: • Nunavut, Iqaluit • Northwest Territories, Yellowknife • Yukon Territory, White Horse	any number
locate	the following geographic locations and understand their importance to the area: • Hudson Bay, Baffin Bay	2
	• Beaufort Sea, Labrador Sea,	2
	• St. Lawrence, Nelson, Saskatchewan Rivers	3
	• Victoria Island	1
compare	Canada, the world's second largest country to the world's largest country, Russia	2
make a table of	information about each province and territory in this country and determine what they have in common:	13
investigate	the who, what, when, where for the following: • Métis • Paul Okalik, Inuit lawyer, Nunavut's first territorial premier • Pierre Elliott Trudeau • Captain Robert Bartlett	4
	the what, when, where, why/how for the following: • Royal Canadian Mounted Police, or Mounties • Bay of Fundy • Canadian Forces Station Alert	4
compare and contrast	a constitutional monarchy with an absolute monarchy	2
research	the history of New Brunswick and the American Revolution loyalists	1
	the Quebec sovereignty movement	1
explain	why three-quarters of Canada's population live within 150 km () of the United States border	1
compare	the three Canada aboriginal peoples • First Nations or Indians • Inuit • Métis	3
graph	8 out of every 10 Canadians live along the Canada/U.S. border	1

Canada

Make a time line of some of the key historic events taking place in this region since 1700:

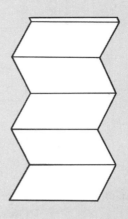

- 1752, Halifax--site of first Canadian newspaper
- 1754-1763, Britain defeated France in French and Indian War, and the territory known as New France became British North America
- 1769, Prince Edward Island (called Saint John's Island until 1799) became a separate colony
- 1770, migration from Scotland to Nova Scotia
- 1774, the Québec Act
- 1776-1780s, Loyalists, and some Native American groups who helped the British, fled to Canada
- 1783, US independent, and the northern part of British North America (Canada), left to the British
- 1837 & 1838, rebellions between Upper and Lower Canada
- 1840-1841, Canadian provinces *Act of Union* created the province of Canada
- 1842, US and Canadian border agreed upon
- 1850-1927, treaties signed with indigenous nations to open their land to settlement
- 1867, Canada became the Dominion of Canada
- 1869, Hudson's Bay Company agreed to sell Canada its northern territories—Rupert's Land and The North-Western Territory—which together became the Northwest Territories
- 1885, transcontinental line completed, extended to present-day Vancouver in 1886
- 1885, the Northwest Rebellion, flared up in 1885
- 1896, gold discovered in Klondike region of Yukon
- 1901, first trans-Atlantic radio transmission received in St. John's, Newfoundland from England
- 1902, indigenous people composed only 2% of the country's population
- 1914-1918, WWI, Britain declared war
- 1929-1930s, Great Depression
- 1931, the British Statute of Westminster--Canada was a sovereign state
- 1939-1945, 42,000 Canadians died in WWII
- 1950-1953, supplied forces to Korean War
- 1957, The Canada Council was founded
- 1970, October Crisis, terrorist FLQ kidnappings
- 1982, gained independence, but British king is still recognized as the ceremonial leader; Canadian Charter of Rights and Freedoms
- 1994, NAFTA, North American Free Trade Agreement
- 1995, voters rejected independence for Quebec
- 1999, Nunavut, new territory created in north
- 2003, Canada decided not to join the U.S.-led coalition against Iraq
- 2007, January passport required for travel between the U.S. and Canada

Time Line

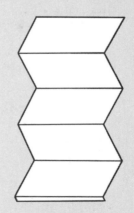

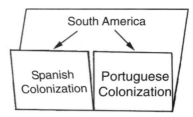

Two-tab concept map

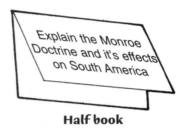

Half book

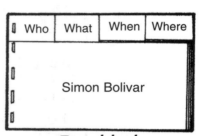

Top-tab book

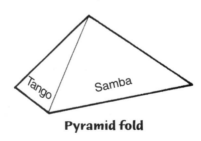

Pyramid fold

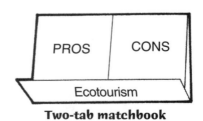

Two-tab matchbook

South America

locate	the following countries and their capital cities on a world map: • Argentina, Buenos Aires • Bolivia, LaPaz and Sucre • Brazil, Brasillia • Chile, Santiago • Colombia, Bogota • Ecuador, Quito • French Guiana, Cayenne • Guyana, Georgetown • Paraguay, Asuncion • Peru, Lima • Suriname, Paramaribo • Uruguay, Montevideo • Venezuela, Caracas	any number
locate	the following geographic locations and understand their importance to the area: • Amazon River and Amazon Basin • Patagonia • Andes Mountains and Aconcagua • Angel Falls, Venezuela • Galapagos Islands • Atacama Desert • Cape Horn • Strait of Magellan • Tierra del Fuego	1
chart	information regarding five countries in this area and determine what they have in common	5
investigate	the who, what, when, where for the following: • Simon Bolivar, Venezuela • Juan and Eva Perón, Argentina • Ché Guevara, Argentina	4
	the what, when, where, why/how for the following: • Carnival, celebrated before Lent begins • PEMEX, Mexico's national oil company • samba, tango, and cumbia • Shining Path, Peru	4
determine	the past and present importance of coffee in Brazil	2
	the effect of the rainforest on Brazil's economy in terms of natural resources and ecotourism	2
compare	the effect of the Great Depression on North America and on South America	2
research	Nationalist movements in Argentina, Brazil, and Mexico during the first half of the 20th century	3
	and report on what economic and political influence the United States has in Latin America	2
describe	what "shanty towns" are and explain why they are often found on the outer fringes of large cities	2
	the impact of eco-tourism in the Galapagos as both benefical and harmful	2
graph	Brazil occupies approximately 47% of South America	1
research	the Isthmus of Panama and its effect on the migration of plants and animals from Central America to South America	1
show cause and effect	of the U.S. Monroe Doctrine and the overthrowing of Chile's government in 1970	2
	how poverty lead to cash crop of coca leaves	2
	oil and politics in Venezuela	2

South America

Make a time line of some of the key historic events taking place in this region since 1800:

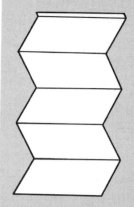

- 1799, a German scientist, Alexander von Humboldt, was given a commission by Spain to thoroughly explore South America (Spanish monarchy hoped to find valuable mineral deposits)
- 1807, Columbia independence movement began in Venezuela, led by Miranda and Bolivar
- 1809, Ecuador independent from Spain
- 1810, Simon Bolivar fought against the Spanish in Venezuela, rebels defeated and Bolivar fled country
- 1812, Bolivar led another expedition to Venezuela
- 1813, Bolivar captured Caracas
- 1816, Congress of Tucuman proclaimed United Provinces of South America against Spain
- 1819, Bolivar's army crossed Andes into New Granada (present-day Columbia)
- 1824, Peru independent from Spain
- 1825, Uruguay independent from Portugal and Spain
- 1830, Venezuela independent from Spanish rule
- 1848-1861, Alfred Wallace, Henry Bates, and Richard Spruce explored and studied the Amazon Basin
- 1908-1935, Venezuela became world's largest exporter of oil
- 1920, US became main investor in Latin America
- 1930, Latin American exports decreased by 50%
- 1933, US announced Good Neighbor Policy (there would be no use of US troops in South America)
- 1938, Getulio Vargas, established New State in Brazil
- 1946, Juan Peron established authoritarian regime in Argentina
- 1948, organization of American states formed
- 1952, Juan Peron, second term as president
- 1954, Brazil president Vargas commited suicide
- 1955, military coup forced Peron into exhile in Paraguay
- 1960, Brazil moved capital from Rio de Janeiro to the new city of Brasilia
- 1966, Guyana independent from Britain
- 1967, Che Guevara died in Bolivia
- 1975, Suriname independent from Dutch
- 1976, General Jorge Videla seized power in Argentina; the "Dirty War" began
- 1981, border war between Peru and Ecuador; resolved through international arbitration
- 1982, Argentine forces occupied Falkland Islands
- 1982, Argentina defeated in U.K. war for Falklands
- 1982, Gabriel Garcia Marquez won Nobel Prize
- 1980s, some countries turned to democratic systems
- 1989, Chile became an independent republic
- 1990s, twenty-nine Latin American cities had populations of over one million
- 1992, Earth Summit held in Rio
- 1993, Peru granted Bolivia a free trade zone in the Peruvian port city of Ilo
- 1999, recession began in Argentina
- 1999, floods and mudslides killed thousands in Venezuela
- 2001, Alejandro Toledo was elected president in Peru
- 2004, Brazil launched first space rocket

Time Line

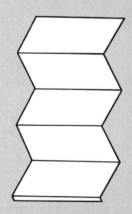

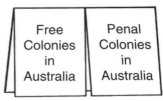
Free Colonies in Australia | Penal Colonies in Australia

Two-tab book

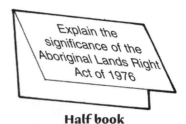
Explain the significance of the Aboriginal Lands Right Act of 1976

Half book

New Zealand North Island | Both | New Zealand South Island

Trifold book

WHAT:
Haka War Dance | WHEN:

WHERE: | WHY/HOW

Four-door book

Australia and New Zealand

locate	the following countries and their capital cities on a world map: • Australia • New Zealand • Island of Tasmania, part of Australia	any number
investigate	the six states and two territories of Australia • New South Wales • Queensland • South Australia • Tasmania • Victoria • Western Australia • Northern Territory • Australian Capital Territory	8
Venn diagram	North Island and South Island of New Zealand	2
locate	the following geographic locations and understand their importance to the area: • Great Barrier Reef • Tasman Sea, Coral Sea, Arafura Sea, Tasman Sea, Great Australian Bight • Indian Ocean • Great Dividing Range of Australia • Southern Alps of New Zealand, Mt. Cook • Ayers Rock, central Australia • Cook Strait	2
make a table of	information about each country in this area and determine what they have in common	3
investigate	the who, what, when, where for the following: • Aborigines • Captain William Bligh, 1806 • Lachlan Macquarie, governor, 1809-1821 • Francis Howard Greenway, (1777-1837), founder of Australian architecture	4
	the what, when, where, why/how for the following: • marsupials • Maoritanga • Sydney Opera House, Australia • dingoes • Norfolk Island • Gallipoli	4
research and report on	the following explorers of Australia: • John Forrest, 1st Baron Forrest, Australian • Charles Sturt, British • Abel Janszoon Tasman, Dutch	any number
locate	the following on a map or globe: • Botany Bay, Australia • Cape York Peninsula, Australia • Bay of Islands, New Zealand • Mount Ruapehu, New Zealand	1
compare	past and present industries--sealing, whaling, wool production	2
determine	what impact squatters, settlers who illegally occupied government lands in order to graze sheep, had on the development of the continent	1
research and sequence events	in the Colonial-Aboriginal War--1788 to 1930	any number

Australia and New Zealand

Make a time line of some of the key historic events taking place in this region since 1800:

- 1770, Cook claimed Australia for Great Britain
- 1787, First Fleet of eleven ships arrived to start penal colony
- 1787, Captain Philip moved the fleet north to Port Jackson, and founded first permanent British settlement on January 26, now known as Australia Day
- 1788-1930, Colonial-Aboriginal Wars (battles, raids, and massacres) began and continued
- 1806, Captain William Bligh and the Rum Rebellion
- 1813, Gregory Blaxland, William Lawson, and William Charles Wentworth crossed the Blue Mountains into western New South Wales
- 1821-1831, Charles Sturt charted interior Australia
- 1824, Hamilton Hume and William Hovell, explorers
- 1836, Thomas Mitchell, explorer
- 1841, New Zealand became separate British colony
- 1845-1848, Maori revolted against British, in NZ
- 1829, Western Australia founded
- 1834, "Tolpuddle Martyrs" transported to Australia
- 1836, South Australia became a British province
- 1837, New Zealand Association formed in London
- 1840, Treaty of Waitangi--Maori and settlers
- 1844-1846, Sturt reached the Simpson Desert
- 1844-1845, Lugwig Leichardt, German explorer, crossed Australia from Bisbane to Gulf of Carpentaria
- 1851, gold discovered at Summer Hill Creek, in New South Wales, settlers moved into Victoria
- 1852, New Zealand Parliament established
- 1852, New South Wales, Victoria, South Australia, and Van Diemen's Land drew up constitutions
- 1852, the British government abolished transporting convicts
- 1856, constitutions approved by British Parliament
- 1856, Van Diemen's Land called Tasmania
- 1859, Queensland became a colony
- 1860, Burke and Wills cross Australia
- 1860-1870, Maori revolts against British rule
- 1871, peace between Maori and British when Maori gained representation in New Zealand Parliament
- 1882, August 29: Australia defeated England at cricket in England for the first time
- 1851, gold discovered in Australian outback
- 1890, Western Australia, constitution approved
- 1893, November 28: New Zealand became world's first country to grant women the right to vote
- 1901, Commonwealth of Australia formed
- 1901, White Australia Policy
- 1914, thousands of troops from New Zealand join allies in WWI, changing the world's opinion of the country
- 1915, Gallipoli, April 15 is Anzac Day, the country's important day of public homage
- 1930, end of Colonial-Aboriginal Wars, (1788-1930)
- 1947, New Zealand became fully independent from Britain
- 1993, the Native Title Act established to grant Aboriginal land rights
- 2000, summer Olympic games at Sydney
- 2004, race riots in Sydney over death of an Aborigine teenager

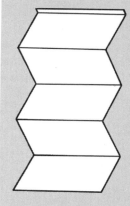

Time Line

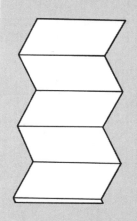

Antarctica and North Pole

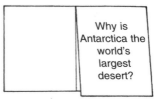

Why is Antarctica the world's largest desert?

Three-quarter book

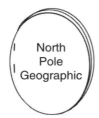

North Pole Geographic

Forward-backward book (front)

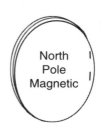

North Pole Magnetic

Forward-backward book (back)

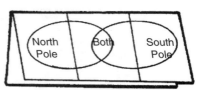

North Pole • Both • South Pole

Three-tab Venn diagram

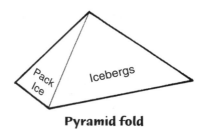

Pack Ice • Icebergs

Pyramid fold

Skill	Activity Suggestion	Foldable Parts
locate	the following on a world map: • Antarctica	1
	North Pole--geographic and magnetic • a point in the Arctic Ocean, usually covered by ice, more than 1600 km (1000 mi) from the geographic North Pole	2
	• South Pole--geographic and magnetic • in central Antarctica, about 2600 km (about 1600 mi) from the south magnetic pole	2
explain	who "owns" or lays claim to each of Earth's polar regions	2
investigate	the who, what, when, where for the explorers of the Arctic: • Roald Amundsen • Robert Abram Bartlett • Vitus Jonassen Bering • Louise Arner Boyd • Frederick Albert Cook • George Washington De Long • Lincoln Ellsworth, Sir John Franklin • Adolphus Washington Greely • Charles Francis Hall • Matthew A. Henson • Elisha Kent Kane • Donald Baxter MacMillan • Fridtjof Nansen • Otto Gustav Nordenskjöld • Adolf Erik Nordenskjöld • Sir William Edward Parry • Robert Edwin Peary • John Rae •Knud Johan •Victor Rasmussen • Naomi Ueura •Sir George Hubert Wilkins	4
	the who, what, when, where of the explorers of the Antarctic: • Roald Amundsen • Fabian Gottlieb von Bellingshausen • Richard Evelyn Byrd • Lincoln Ellsworth • Sir Vivian Ernest Fuchs • Sir Edmund Percival Hillary • Sir Douglas Mawson • Otto Gustav Nordenskjöld • Robert Falcon Scott • Sir Ernest Henry Shackleton • Sir George Hubert Wilkins	4
investigate	the what, when, where, why/how for the following: • atomic submarine Nautilus • dogsledding • Samoyed (dog breed used by Arctic explorers) • northern passage to Asia	4
locate	the following geographic locations and understand their importance to the area: • Transantarctic Mountains, Vinson Massif highest peak • South Pole • Mount Erebus, active volcano • Greenland ice cap	1
make a Venn diagram	to compare the North Pole, South Pole, both	3
compare	a regular compass and a gyrocompass	2
	icebergs, pack ice, and glaciers	3
make a time line	of some of the key historic events: • 1909, Peary, Henson, four Inuit reached North Pole • 1911, Amundson reached the South Pole • 1912, January: Captain Scotts party reached the South Pole thirty-four days after Amundson's, perishes on return • 1926, Roald Amundsen flies over the North Pole • 1929, Byrd and Bennett flew over the South Pole • 1935, first flight across Antarctica, Lincoln Ellsworth • 1958, US atomic submarine Nautilus was the first sub to pass under the ice covering the North Pole • 1978, Naomi Uemura, Japanese fist solo trek to NP • Antarctic Treaty System, international treaties to conserve and protect Antarctica	any number

Oceania

locate	the following countries and their capital cities on a world map: • American Somoa, Pago Pago • Federated States of Micronesia, Palikir • Fiji Islands, Suva • French Polynesia, Papeete capital on island of Tahiti • Guam, Hagatñá • Kiribati, Tarawa • Marshall Islands, Majuro • Northern Mariana Islands, Saipan • Nauru, Yaren • New Caledonia, Noumea • Palau, Koror • Papua New Guinea, Port Moresby • Pitcairn Islands, Adamstown • Samoa, Apia • Solomon Islands, Honiara • Tokelau, each atoll has own administrative center • Tonga, Nuku'alofa • Tuvalu, Funafuti • Vanuatu, Port-Vila • Wallis and Futuna, Matâ' Utu	any number
research	the three island regions of Oceania: Melanesia, Micronesia, and Polynesia	3
compare	high islands and low island (atolls)	2
determine	how sonar technology aided ocean exploration	2
make a table	of information about five countries in this area and determine what they have in common	5
investigate	the who, what, when, where for the following: • Dumont d'Urville, French explorer • Padre San Vitores, Spanish missionary	4
	the what, when, where, why/how for the following: • oceanography as a science • *HMS Challenger*,(1872-1876) • the Mau movement • maoi, Easter Island statues • Bikini Atoll	4
research and report on	the following South Seas explorers: • Captain James Cook, British • Antoine Raymond Joseph de Bruni, French • Chevalier d'Entrecasteaux, French	3
outline	ancient to modern shipbuilding methods	any number
locate	the following geographic locations and understand their importance to the area: • South Pacific Ocean • International Date Line	1
make a time line and include key events in the history of other island countries	of some of the key historic events taking place in this region on Fiji, Guam, and Papua New Guinea: • 1521, Ferdinand Magellan claimed Guam for Spain • 1545, Inigo Ortiz de Retes named an island New Guinea because he thought the islanders looked like those along the Guinea coast of Africa • 1565, Guam annexed by Spain • 1643 Dutch explorer Abel Tasman, first European to sight Fiji islands • 1840s, the first maps of Fiji made by Charles Wilkes • 1898, Treaty of Paris ceded by Spain to the US • 1941, Guam captured by Japan • 1944, Guam retaken by US forces • 1950, people of Guam became US citizens • 1970, Fiji became independent, member of UN • 1973, Papua and New Guinea became self governing as Papua New Guinea and independent, 1975 • 1992, Guam devastated by Typhoon Omar	any number

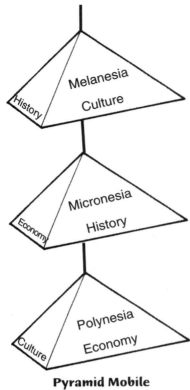

Pyramid Mobile

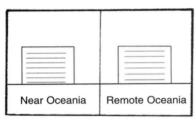

Pocket book

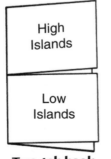

Two-tab book

World History
Reproducible
Graphics

Auschwitz

Alexander the Great

Aquaducts

Assyria

Buddha

Napoleon Bonaparte

Ludwig Von Beethoven

Johann Sebastion Bach

Julius Caesar

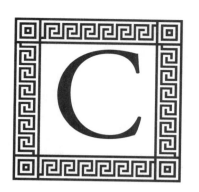

Cuniform

Marie Curie

The Crusades

D

Dead Sea Scrolls

Leonardo Da Vinci

Charles Darwin

Charles De Gaul

Easter Island

Queen Elizabeth I

Eiffel Tower

Egyptian Pyramids

F

Fire

Anne Frank

Frederick the Great

Fiefdom

Great Wall of China

Guillotine

Mohandas Ghandi

Galileo Galilei

Hindenburg

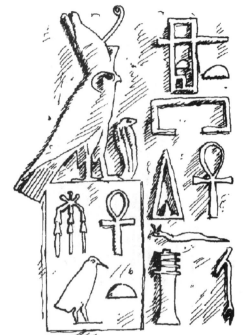

Heiroglyphics

Henry VIII

Ho Chi Minh

Industrial Revolution

Inca

Ireland

Islamic Mosque

J

Japan

Joan of Arc

Judaism

Chinese Junk

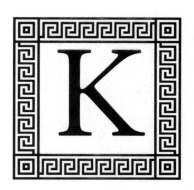

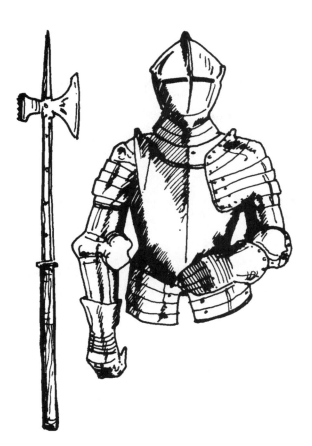

Knight

Khmer

Jomo Kenyatta

Korean War

Charles Lindberg

Vladimir Lenin

Martin Luther

Louis XIV

Ho Chi Minh

Mesopotamia

Marco Polo

Mycenae

Nomads

Nazi Germany

Alfred Nobel

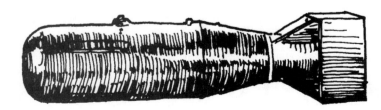

Nuclear Bomb

Olympics

Osiris

Octavian Augustus

Olmec

P

Paleolithic Period

Pisa, Italy

Parthenon

Plague

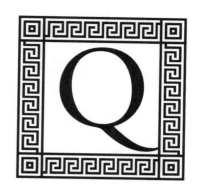

Qur'an

Quinine

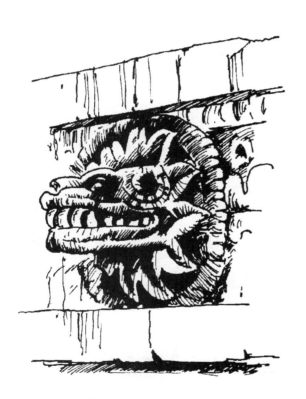

Quetzalcoatl

Emperor Qin

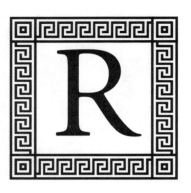

Roman Colosseum

Renaissance

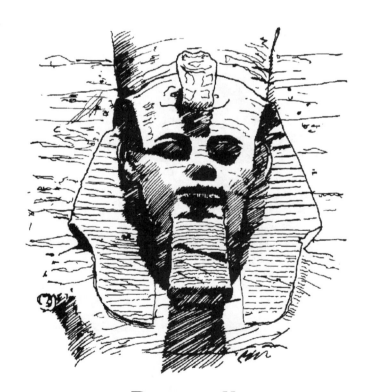

Ramses II

**Roman
Sculpture**

Stonehenge

Stone Age Tools

Joseph Stalin

William Shakespeare

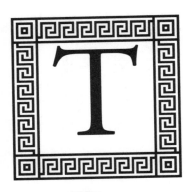

Taj Mahal

Toltecs

Titanic

Trojan War

United Nations

United Kingdom

U-Boat

Queen Victoria

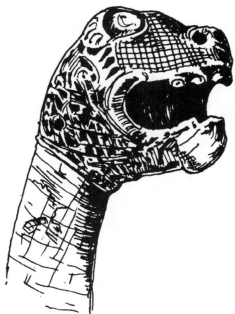

Vikings

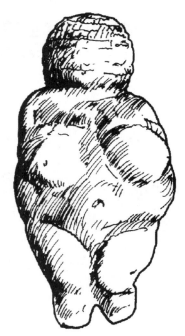

Venus of Willendorf

Vlad the Impaler

WW II

Kaiser Wilhelm II

Windmill

WW I

St. Francis Xavier

Xochiquetzal

Xerxes I

Malcolm X

Yalta Conference

Yuri Gagarin

Boris Yeltsin

Yucatan

Zapotec

Emiliano Zapata

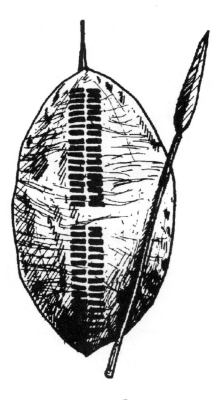

Zulu

Ziggurat

Generic Time Lines

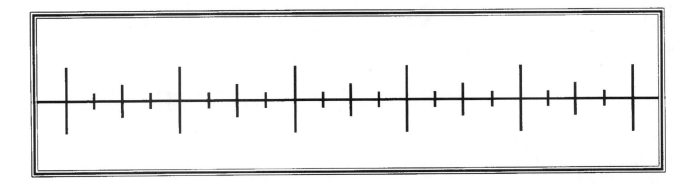

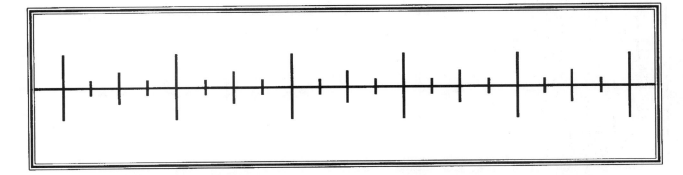

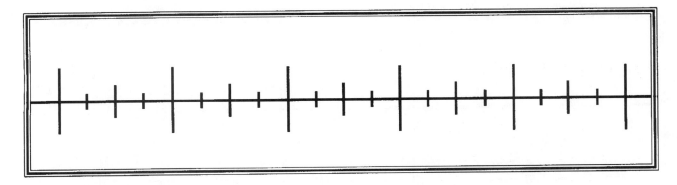

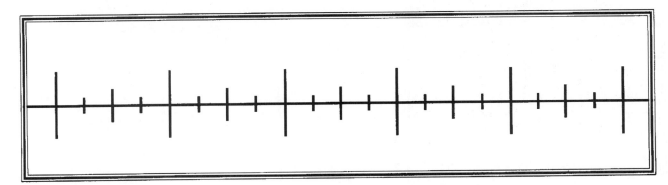

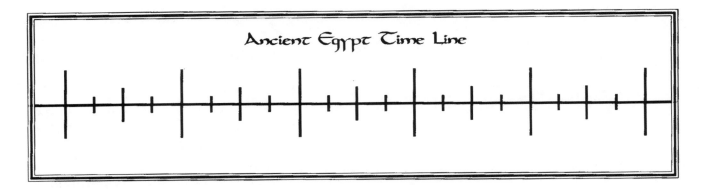

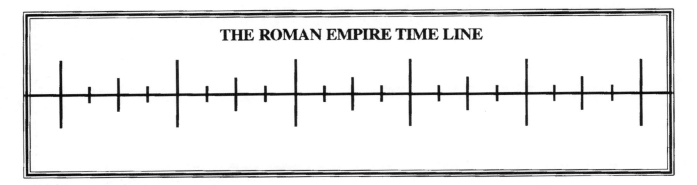

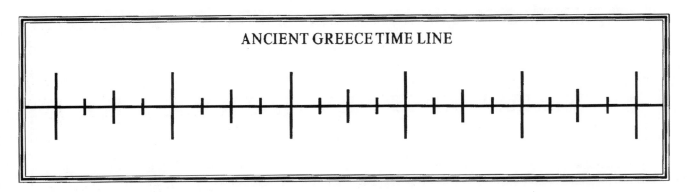

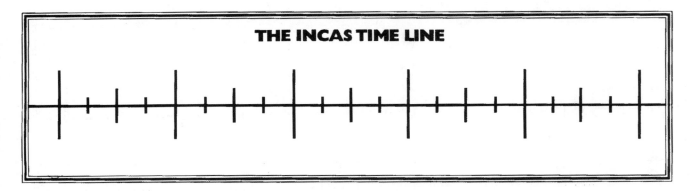

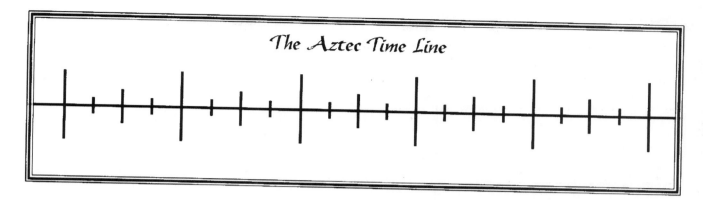

The Aztec Time Line

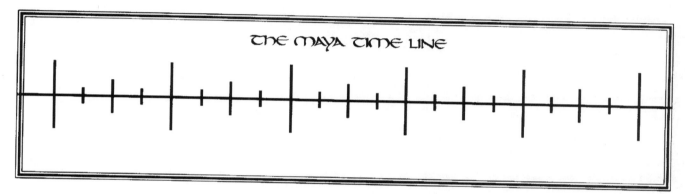

THE MAYA TIME LINE

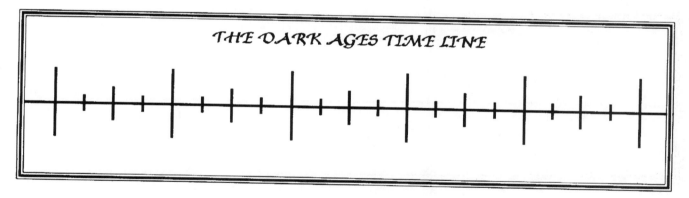

THE DARK AGES TIME LINE

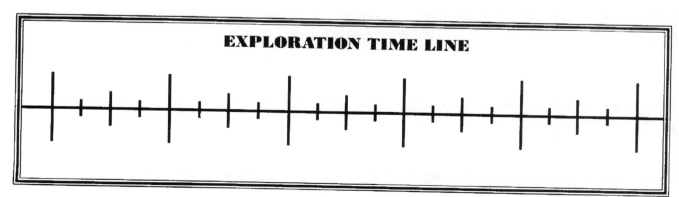

EXPLORATION TIME LINE

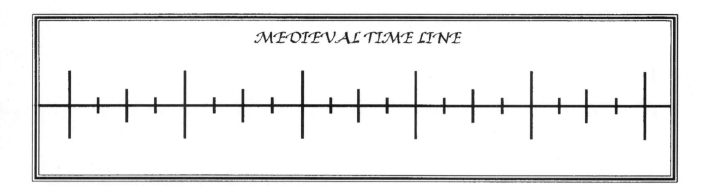

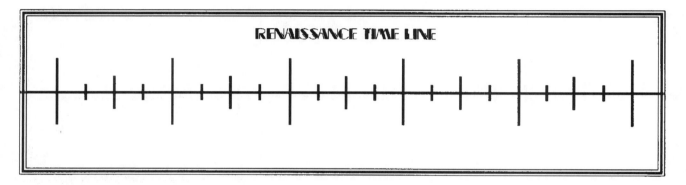

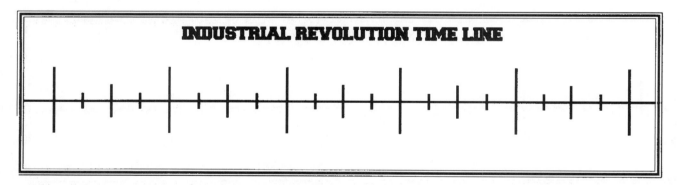

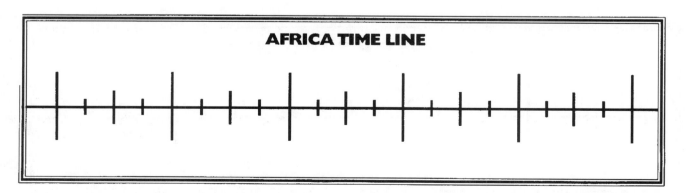

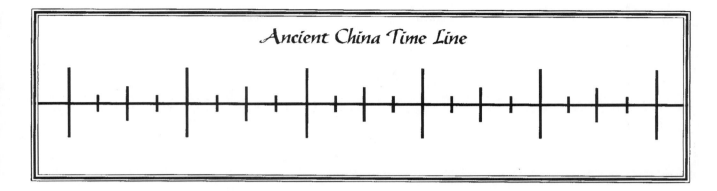

Ancient China Time Line

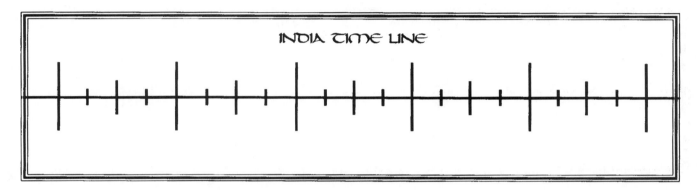

INDIA TIME LINE

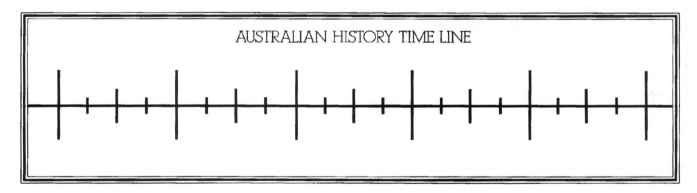

AUSTRALIAN HISTORY TIME LINE

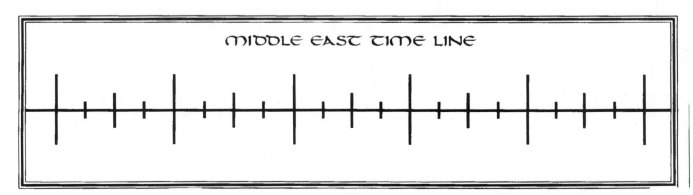

MIDDLE EAST TIME LINE

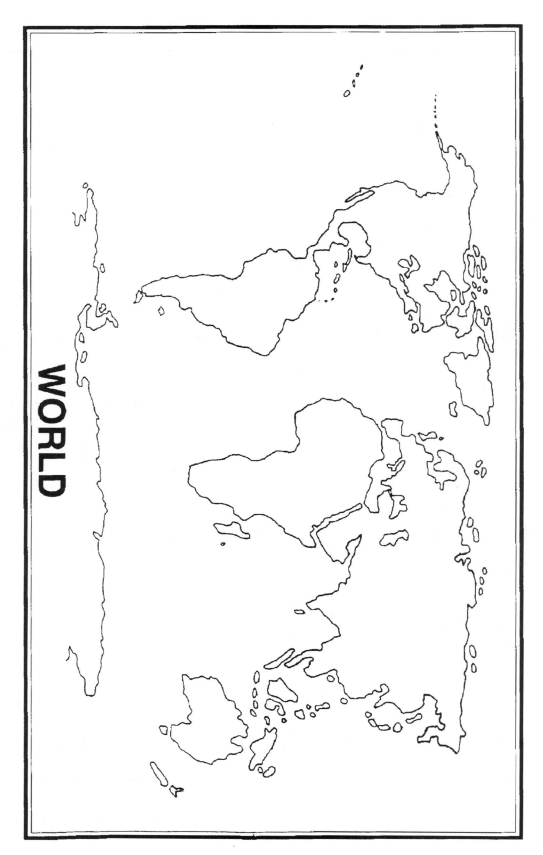

WORLD

Africa

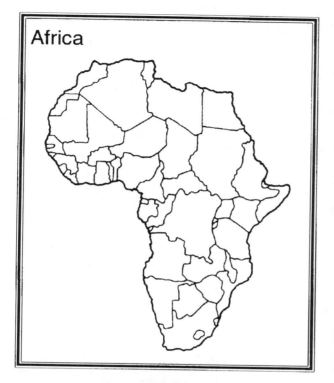

Antarctica

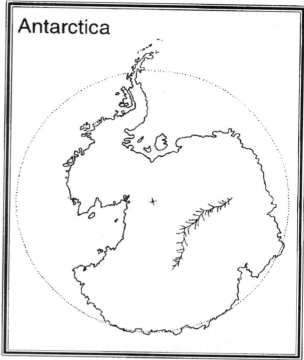

Asia

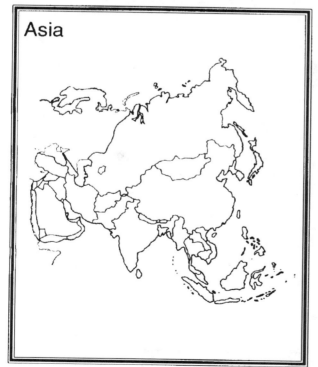

Australia

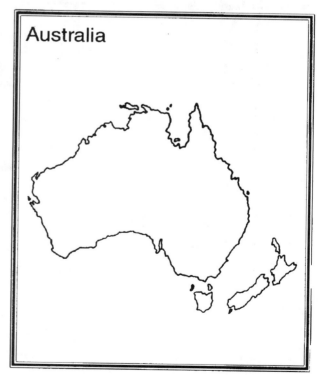

Europe

North America

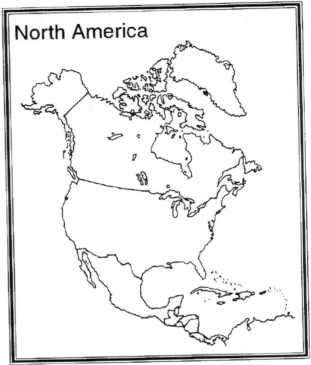

South America

World

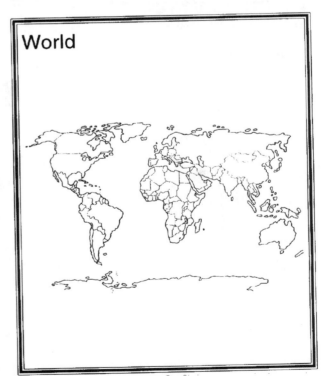

Europe

Antarctica

Africa

Asia

Australia

North America

South America

Index

Index

Workshops
and Keynote Presentations

Dinah's presentations give participants an unprecedented opportunity to meet and work with the designer as she shares her internationally renowned, three-dimensional, interactive graphic organizers. Teachers learn how to make class work, projects, assessment, and note taking unforgettable visual and kinesthetic experiences. Dinah's Foldables™ can be used by students and teachers in all grade levels and subjects.

Workshops

For more information on Dinah Zike's workshops and keynote presentations, contact Jeanne Herbs at **1-210-698-0123** or **jeanne@dinah.com**.

Orders

To receive a free catalog or to order other books by Dinah Zike, call **1-800-99DINAH** or email at **orders@dinah.com**.

E-Group

To join Dinah Zike's e-group and receive new activity ideas, send an email to **mindy@dinah.com** or sign up on our website at **www.dinah.com**.

Watch for new and upcoming books in
Dinah Zike's Big Book series!

Each book in Dinah's Big Book series is subject specific and features instructions for approximately thirty graphic organizers, 100 full-color photographed examples, five black-line art examples per page, and thousands of graphic organizer ideas for teaching.

Please check our website at www.dinah.com or call 210-698-0123 for availability of books for the following subjects:

Elementary
Dinah Zike's Big Book of...
Social Studies (K-6)
Texas History (K-7)
Math (K-6)
Foldables and V-K-V's for Phonics, Vocabulary, and Spelling (PreK-2)
Foldables and V-K-V's for Phonics, Vocabulary, and Spelling (3rd-6th)

Middle School and High School
Dinah Zike's Big Book of...
Science (7-12)
Math (7-12)
Texas History (K-7)
American History (7-12)
World History (7-12)
Foldables and V-K-V's for Phonics, Vocabulary, and Spelling (MS/HS)
Foldables and V-K-V's for Grammar: Primary to Advanced